RECENT WETLAND STATUS AND TRENDS IN THE CHESAPEAKE WATERSHED (1982 TO 1989): TECHNICAL REPORT

by

Ralph W. Tiner, Irene Kenenski,
Todd Nuerminger, John Eaton,
David B. Foulis, Glenn S. Smith, and W. Edward Frayer

U.S. Fish and Wildlife Service
Ecological Services
300 Westgate Center Drive
Hadley, MA 01035

Prepared for the Chesapeake Bay Program

May 1994

The recommendations contained in this report are the opinions of the authors and do not necessarily reflect the opinion of the Chesapeake Bay Program, nor any other group or agency associated with this program.

Printed by the U.S. Environmental Protection Agency for the Chesapeake Bay Program

U.S. Fish and Wildlife Service
Chesapeake Bay Field Office
177 Admiral Cochrane Drive
Annapolis, MD 21401

U.S. Environmental Protection Agency
Chesapeake Bay Program Office
410 Severn Avenue
Annapolis, MD 21403

Copies of this report may be obtained from: Chesapeake Bay Program, 410 Severn Avenue, Suite 109, Annapolis, Maryland 21403, telephone: (800) 968-7229 or U.S. Fish and Wildlife Service, 177 Admiral Cochrane Drive, Annapolis, Maryland 21401, telephone: (410-224-2732).

This report should be cited as follows:

Tiner, R.W., I. Kenenski, T. Nuerminger, D.B. Foulis, J. Eaton, G.S. Smith, and W.E. Frayer. 1994. Recent Wetland Status and Trends in the Chesapeake Watershed (1982 to 1989): Technical Report. U.S. Fish and Wildlife Service, Region 5, Ecological Services, Hadley, MA. Cooperative interagency technical report prepared for the Chesapeake Bay Program, Annapolis, MD. 70 pp. plus appendices.

TABLE OF CONTENTS

LIST OF TABLES

LIST OF FIGURES

iv

ACKNOWLEDGMENTS

The authors wish to express their thanks to the following persons for assisting in the completion of this study. Dr. Ed Pendleton of the U.S. Fish and Wildlife Service and Carin Bisland of the U.S. Environmental Protection Agency served as project officers for this project. Funding support for this study came from the Chesapeake Bay Program through the U.S. Fish and Wildlife Service and the U.S. Environmental Protection Agency.

Dr. Donald Woodard, Group Leader of the U.S. Fish and Wildlife Service's National Wetlands Inventory Group (NWI) and his staff, especially Becky Stanley, Linda Shaffer, and Tom Dahl, provided help in obtaining aerial photography, plotting work areas, accessing existing national trend plot files, and coordinating activities with NWI's support service contractor. Doug Cribbs and his staff at GEONEX, Inc. were responsible for scan digitizing all trend plot information and georeferencing all plots; they also assisted in trend photointerpretation near the end of the project. Pam Dansereau and Chris Nolan of the U.S. Fish and Wildlife Service provided invaluable technical support in manuscript typing and desktop publishing, and data tabulation, respectively.

We also wish to acknowledge reviewers of the draft manuscript. Their comments helped us reformat the report and cull out the pertinent facts. Reviewers were Steven Funderburk (U.S. Fish and Wildlife Service), Frank Dawson and Mike Slattery (Maryland Water Resources Administration), Stephen Capel (Virginia Department of Game and Inland Fisheries), Collin Powers (Virginia Department of Environmental Quality), Ken Reisinger (Pennsylvania Department of Environmental Resources), and Elizabeth Zucker (Chesapeake Bay Foundation). Vivian Newman provided information on public attitudes toward wetlands that is referenced in this report. In addition, discussions with the Wetlands Work Group of the Living Resources Subcommittee (the Chesapeake Bay Program) were also helpful in producing this report.

INTRODUCTION

Chesapeake Bay is the Nation's largest estuary and perhaps the best studied and arguably the most politically visible one. It is noted for its productive fisheries and shellfisheries (e.g., blue crabs and oysters), water-borne commerce, and vast recreational opportunities for boating, fishing, waterfowl hunting, and nature observation. Despite these widely recognized values, the quality of the Bay's waters has significantly deteriorated since the 1950s (Schubel 1986). Harvests of blue crabs and oysters have declined and numbers of striped bass or rockfish have decreased to the point that rigid catch restrictions have been established for the fishery. The reason for this degradation of the Bay and decline of its living resources is complicated by many factors, but undoubtedly increasing urban development, other land-use changes (e.g., conversion of forests to cropland), and poor land management practices throughout the Watershed have significantly contributed to the problem. Point source water pollution from urban centers (e.g., Baltimore, Hampton, Norfolk, Richmond, and Washington), nonpoint source pollution (e.g., runoff of agrochemicals and dairy wastes from agricultural lands and fertilizers from suburban lawns), channelization and dredging projects, and wetland destruction have all led to the Bay's deterioration. More than 13 million people live within the Watershed draining into Chesapeake Bay (Schubel 1986).

Loss of wetlands eliminates valuable natural functions, such as water quality improvement, shoreline stabilization, and flood water storage, that are provided free of charge to society. While individual wetlands may seem insignificant to some people, wetlands function as an integrated system, especially in water quality improvement and flood water retention. Loss of a seemingly small, but critical, amount of wetland may destroy the integrity of the entire system and greatly impair its functional capacity. In terms of wetland functions, the system is greater than the sum of its parts. Functional losses of individual wetlands or parts of wetlands throughout the Watershed and its subbasins therefore exacerbate the overall decline in the Bay's water quality and adversely affect its living resources. Knowledge of wetland status and trends in the Watershed is critically important to developing public policy and strategies for improving the quality of Chesapeake Bay and restoring its living resources.

Public support for wetland protection and concern about wetland destruction has steadily increased in recent years. Most Americans believe that not enough is being done to protect our remaining wetlands (e.g., Environment Opinion Survey 1991; Harris 1982). Wetlands are now considered one of the Nation's most treasured natural resources, not only because they provide habitat for unique and interesting wildlife, but perhaps mostly due to the public services they provide (e.g., water quality improvement, flood storage, and shoreline stabilization). Government and private initiatives ranging from regulatory programs (e.g., Federal Clean Water Act) to public and private wetland restoration efforts have steadily improved the status of some wetlands in the Chesapeake Watershed since the 1970s.

In the Chesapeake Watershed, significant progress has been made in strengthening wetland protection. In the 1970s, Maryland and Virginia passed laws to protect tidal wetlands and regulate construction activities in these areas. Tidal wetlands along the Nanticoke River in Delaware have also been protected since 1973 under Delaware's Tidal Wetland Act. Activities in inland (nontidal) wetlands are also regulated by some states. In 1975, New York passed the first wetland protection act affecting inland wetlands in the Chesapeake Watershed, while Pennsylvania (1979) and Maryland (1989) enacted similar state legislation more recently. Virginia and Delaware have yet to enact laws to protect nontidal wetlands. Virginia has, however, established a program to enhance protection of nontidal wetlands through Section 401 of the Federal Clean Water Act. Delaware is considering initiatives to protect these wetlands to some degree. At the Federal level, certain activities in both tidal and nontidal wetlands throughout the Watershed are regulated by the U.S. Army Corps of Engineers in accordance with the Federal Clean Water Act and the Rivers and Harbors Act. Since the mid-70s, there has been increased regulation of wetlands in the Watershed. With this, we should anticipate a noticeable decline in the loss of wetlands due to certain human impacts over the rate that occurred prior to strengthened wetland protection.

In the mid-1980s, the U.S. Fish and Wildlife Service (FWS), Region 5 and the U.S. Environmental Protection Agency (EPA), Region III wanted reliable estimates on the status and trends of wetlands in five states: Delaware, Maryland, Pennsylvania, Virginia, and West Virginia. With EPA funding, the FWS conducted a statistical study of wetland trends to accomplish this objective. This study provided estimates of the status and trends of wetlands in the five states, including the majority of the Chesapeake Watershed, from the mid-1950s to the late 1970s/early 1980s. Study findings were reported in two major publications (Tiner and Finn 1986; Tiner 1987).

In 1987, the Living Resources Subcommittee of the Chesapeake Bay Program was formed to restore and protect the Bay's living resources, their habitats and ecological relationships. The Living Resources Subcommittee subsequently developed numerous resource-specific management plans for the restoration of Chesapeake Bay's living resources. The Wetlands Policy Implementation Plan calls for monitoring the status and trends of wetlands in the Watershed every 5 years. The Subcommittee selected the National Wetlands Inventory unit of Fish and Wildlife Service's Northeast Regional Office, Ecological Services (FWS-ES) to accomplish this.

In 1992, the Chesapeake Bay Program allocated funds to FWS-ES to initiate a two-phased effort to assess wetland trends in the Chesapeake Watershed for the early 1980s to the late 80s/early 90s. Phase I of the study used statistical sampling procedures to generate estimates of wetland status and trends in the 63,000-square mile Chesapeake Watershed for the study period. This technical report presents significant findings of this study for the Chesapeake Watershed. Phase II of the effort involved conducting detailed wetland trends studies in selected areas. These areas were chosen by FWS and EPA field personnel, in consultation with state officials. As such, the Phase II study areas represent areas with potentially heavy threats to wetlands or other areas of interest to these agencies. The results of the Phase II studies are published in a series of technical reports (see Appendices A and B for list of these references and highlights of each study). In addition to the above reports, a 12-page executive summary report entitled "Recent Wetland Status and Trends in the Chesapeake Watershed (1982 to 1989): Executive Summary Report" (Tiner 1994) has been published and is available.

Organization of this Report

The report is organized into sections: (1) Introduction, (2) Methods, (3) Interpretation of Results, (4) Results for the Watershed, (5) Results by State, (6) Wetland Loss Hotspots, (7) Discussion, and (8) Conclusions and Recommendations. References cited in the text and a glossary are provided at the back of the text along with two appendices that present additional data on wetland trends in the Chesapeake Watershed.

METHODS

The study involved three basic steps: (1) study design, (2) data collection, and (3) data compilation and analysis. Each step is discussed in the subsections following the study area description.

Study Area

The study area is the drainage system for Chesapeake Bay. The Chesapeake Watershed encompasses approximately 63,000-square miles of surface area in six states: Virginia, Maryland, Delaware, Pennsylvania, West Virginia, and New York (Figure 1). Over 150 rivers and streams drain into Chesapeake Bay (Schubel 1986). Major rivers in the Chesapeake Watershed include the Susquehanna, Juniata, Potomac, Chester, Pocomoke, Nanticoke, Patuxent, Choptank, James, Rappahannock, Appomattox, Pamunkey, Mattaponi, and York. Chesapeake Bay is the largest estuary in the United States.

The Watershed falls within several physiographic provinces. These landscape areas are defined as Hammond's land surface forms (Hammond 1970) or the provinces of Fenneman (1928) (see Table 1 for the correlation between Fenneman and Hammond). The majority (61 percent; about 38,000-square miles) of the Watershed is in the Appalachian Highlands, with 30 percent (about 19,000-square miles) in the Rolling Plain and 9 percent in the Coastal Flats (about 5,000-square miles). The abundance, diversity, and characteristics of wetlands is directly related to these land forms.

The upper part of the Chesapeake Watershed was covered by the Wisconsin glaciation which receded 10-12,000 years ago. This event had a profound influence on wetland distribution by increasing the number of wetlands in this portion of the Watershed over that in the nonglaciated portion of the Appalachian Highlands. It also affected coastal wetlands, since the Atlantic coast shoreline was nearly 100 miles offshore of its current location and at an elevation roughly 300 feet lower than the current level during the last glaciation (Wolfe 1977). About 10,000 years ago, the melting of continental glaciers caused sea levels to rise dramatically, inundating the former coastal plain (now the continental shelf) and reaching the mouth of present day Chesapeake Bay (Schubel 1986). The seas continued to rise drowning the lower Susquehanna River basin, and eventually sea levels stabilized about 3,000 years ago to form Chesapeake Bay as we know it today. At this point, tidal wetlands began forming along the Bay's shorelines in areas of heavy sediment accumulation. Once established, most of these marshes were able to keep pace with slower rates of sea level rise that followed.

Study Design

Statistical sampling techniques are proven methods for estimating national and regional wetland status and trends. National wetland trends studies and the original regional wetland trends study which included the Chesapeake Watershed used a stratified random sampling technique where four-square mile plots were selected for sampling (Dahl and Johnson 1991, Frayer 1991, Frayer, et al. 1983, Tiner and Finn 1986). The same study design was used in

Figure 1.   The Chesapeake Watershed.

Table 1. Correlation between Hammond's physical subdivisions (Hammond 1970) used in this study and the more familiar types of Fenneman (1928) found in the Watershed.

Hammond's Physical Subdivisions	Fenneman Divisions
Appalachian Highlands	Appalachian Plateau, Valley and Ridge, and Blue Ridge
Gulf-Atlantic Rolling Plain - Irregular Plains	Upper Coastal Plain
Gulf-Atlantic Rolling Plain	Upper Coastal Plain and Piedmont
Gulf-Atlantic Coastal Flats	Lower Coastal Plain

the present study for obvious reasons, including: (1) it was a proven technique for sampling wetland changes that was immediately available for our use, (2) existing plot data from the most recent national wetland trends study could be utilized for the present study, thereby avoiding duplication of effort, and (3) existing plots within the Chesapeake Watershed from the previous regional wetland trends study could be utilized and re-sampled.

The initial sampling strata for this study were derived from state boundaries, physical subdivisions described by Hammond (1970), and the coastal zone boundary (marine and estuarine systems). In the Chesapeake Watershed, there were six state boundaries (Delaware, Maryland, New York, Pennsylvania, Virginia, and West Virginia), three physical subdivisions (Gulf-Atlantic Coastal Flats, Gulf-Atlantic Rolling Plain, and Appalachian Highlands), and coastal zone boundaries for Maryland and Virginia, comprising a total of 12 strata.

Based on previous work in five Mid-Atlantic states by Tiner and Finn (1986), further stratification was warranted to improve sampling efficiency. A total of 22 strata were established for the Chesapeake Watershed (Table 2 and Figure 2). The additional strata were largely established due to differences in wetland abundance within a particular physiographic region. Such stratification should improve sampling efficiency and lower the number of samples required to produce acreage estimates of wetland types with a certain level of reliability. The Coastal Zone stratum was divided into two strata: (1) Coastal Deep Water Zone (waters deeper than 10m) and (2) Coastal Intertidal/Shallow Water Zone. The latter stratum is where estuarine wetlands exist and are likely to establish, whereas the former stratum contains only estuarine deepwater habitats, requiring only minimal sampling. One additional stratum was added to the present study design: Southeast Virginia Metro Area. This is an area of high wetland density and considerable wetland development pressure. It was identified as a wetland loss "hotspot" by Tiner (1987).

Table 2. Regional sampling strata for the Chesapeake Watershed. Most of the strata were derived from Hammond's physical subdivisions (1970), with some smaller areas of interest also identified. More familiar of the major physiographic regions (Fenneman 1928) are shown in parentheses. An asterisk (*) denotes strata containing the majority of estuarine waters and wetlands which is represented by the Coastal Zone stratum in the national study.

State	Stratum
Delaware	Gulf-Atlantic Coastal Flats (Lower Coastal Plain) Pothole Region - subset of Coastal Flats stratum
Maryland	Coastal Intertidal/Shallow Water Zone* Coastal Deep Water Zone* Gulf-Atlantic Coastal Flats (Lower Coastal Plain) Pothole Region - subset of Coastal Flats stratum Gulf-Atlantic Rolling Plain #2 - Irregular Plains (Upper Coastal Plain) Gulf-Atlantic Rolling Plain #1 (Piedmont) Appalachian Highlands (includes Appalachian Plateau, Valley and Ridge, and Blue Ridge)
New York	Appalachian Highlands
Pennsylvania	Appalachian Highlands (includes most of Appalachian Plateau, Valley and Ridge, and Blue Ridge) Poconos #1 - subset of Appalachian Highlands Poconos #2 - subset of Appalachian Highlands Other Glaciated - subset of Appalachian Highlands
Virginia	Coastal Intertidal/Shallow Water Zone* Coastal Deep Water Zone* Gulf-Atlantic Coastal Flats (Lower Coastal Plain) Southeast Virginia Metro Area - subset of the Coastal Flats stratum Gulf-Atlantic Rolling Plain #2 (Upper Coastal Plain) Gulf-Atlantic Rolling Plain #1 (Piedmont) Appalachian Highlands (includes Appalachian Plateau, Valley and Ridge, and Blue Ridge)
West Virginia	Appalachian Highlands (includes Appalachian Plateau and Valley and Ridge)

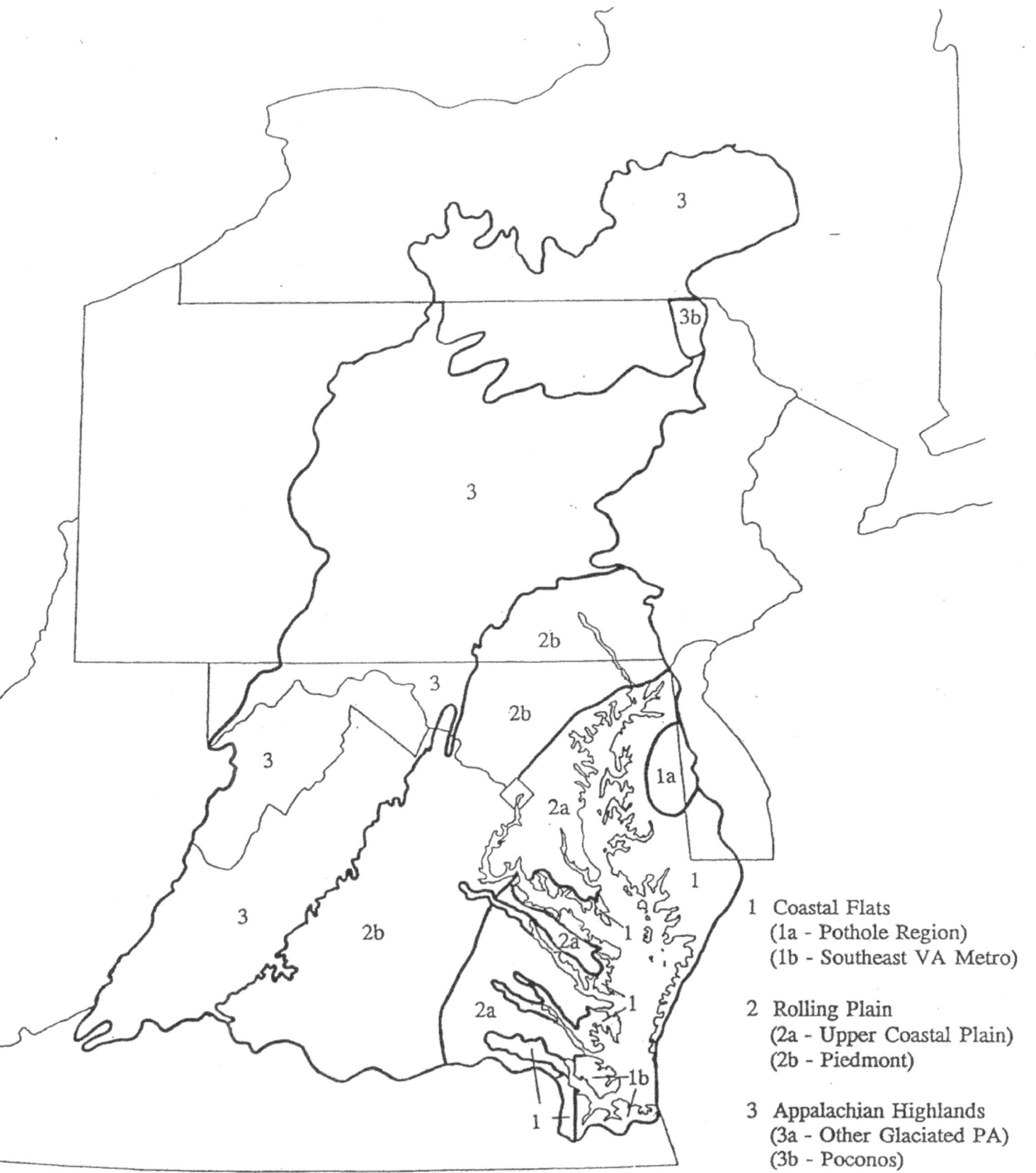

Figure 2. **General location of Watershed sampling strata.**
(Note: The Coastal Zone stratum is not shown due to intricate shoreline detail;
it essentially follows the shoreline of Chesapeake Bay and its brackish water
tributaries).

1 Coastal Flats
(1a - Pothole Region)
(1b - Southeast VA Metro)

2 Rolling Plain
(2a - Upper Coastal Plain)
(2b - Piedmont)

3 Appalachian Highlands
(3a - Other Glaciated PA)
(3b - Poconos)

Sample Plots

The goal of the statistical sampling program was to estimate the totals for each major vegetated wetland type in the Watershed with a standard error of less than 20 percent of the mean. To accomplish this, all previous plots in the Watershed sampled during the previous study by Tiner and Finn (1986) needed to be re-examined. In addition, new plots needed to be added to certain strata to improve statistics (lower the variance). Existing plots were located and then the sampling grids used in these studies were reconstructed. The desired number of new plots for each stratum in the Watershed were located by random sampling, without replacement.

The basic sample unit was a 4-square mile plot covering 2,560 acres. When a plot fell in two or more strata, the plot was divided into split plots for analysis. Table 3 shows the number of plots sampled within each stratum. A total of 760 plots were analyzed.

Data Collection

The type and extent of wetlands within each sample plot were determined through conventional aerial photointerpretation techniques. Aerial photographs from the early 80s and late 80s/early 90s were obtained for each plot. Based on the photos analyzed, the mean study period was 1982 to 1989, for a study interval of seven years. Wetlands were defined and classified using the U.S. Fish and Wildlife Service's (FWS) wetland classification system (Cowardin, et al. 1979).

Wetlands were classified to system, subsystem, and class, with modifiers applied for timber harvest (forested wetlands only), ditching, and beaver-influence. This FWS wetland definition includes both vegetated wetlands and nonvegetated wetlands (e.g., mud flats and rocky shores). The vegetated wetlands were equivalent to those identified using the Federal Interagency Wetland Delineation Manual (Federal Interagency Committee for Wetland Delineation 1989). Wetland categories and other habitats and land types classified during the study are briefly defined in Table 4.

Existing National Wetlands Inventory (NWI) maps derived from color infrared aerial photos were used as the basis to record the current location of wetlands, with improvements made through examination of aerial photos. When these maps were not available (e.g., maps based on black and white photographs), recent color infrared aerial photography (i.e., 1:58,000 or 1:40,000) was interpreted. Improvements or enhancements based on re-examination of the original NWI photointerpretation were added to the wetland status overlay prior to performing trends analysis. *This means that more wetland acreage was present in 1982 than the former study by Tiner and Finn (1986) had estimated.* The minimum mapping unit was approximately one-quarter to one-half acre. Wetlands delineated in each plot were then compared with the 1989-era, 1:40,000 color infrared photos to detect changes in wetland boundaries and/or cover types. The causes of change, either natural or human-induced (i.e., agriculture, urbanization, or other factors; see Table 4) were also identified. A wetland overlay was prepared using a Bausch & Lomb stereo zoom transfer scope or similar

10

Table 3. Number of plots sampled within the Chesapeake Watershed. Area of each stratum is also presented.

Region/State	Stratum	Area of Stratum in Square Miles	Number of Plots
Delaware	Pothole Region	196	5
	Remaining Coastal Flats	513	23
	(Subtotal)	(709)	(28)
Maryland	Appalachian Highlands	1,339	19
	Rolling Plain #1	2,574	33
	Rolling Plain #2	2,095	28
	Pothole Region	473	11
	Remaining Coastal Flats	2,263	96
	Coastal Zone	2,275	147
	(Subtotal)	(11,019)	(334)
New York	Appalachian Highlands	6,181	*4
	(Subtotal)	(6,181)	(4)
Pennsylvania	Poconos #1	43	7
	Poconos #2	337	24
	Other Glaciated	3,411	20
	Remaining Appalachian Highlands	16,252	47
	Rolling Plain	2,435	29
	(Subtotal)	(22,478)	(127)
Virginia	Appalachian Highlands	7,244	26
	Rolling Plain #1	9,057	38
	Rolling Plain #2	3,096	28
	Southeast Metro Area	666	29
	Remaining Coastal Flats	1,296	49
	Coastal Zone	1,536	81
	(Subtotal)	(22,895)	(251)
West Virginia	Appalachian Highlands	3,571	16
	(Subtotal)	(3,571)	(16)
Chesapeake Watershed	Coastal Zone	3,811	228
	Coastal Flats	5,407	213
	Rolling Plain	19,257	156
	Appalachian Highlands	38,378	163
	Total for Watershed (includes Bay acreage)	66,853	760
	Total excluding Coastal Zone	63,042	532

*Limited plots due to lack of adequate aerial photos for study period.

Table 4. Categories used for wetland trends analysis.

Category (Code)	Brief Description
Estuarine Subtidal Habitat (E1UB)	Saltwater deepwater habitats (e.g., open water and bay bottoms; coastal rivers)
Estuarine Emergent Wetland (E2EM)	Salt and brackish tidal marshes
Estuarine Scrub-Shrub Wetland (E2SS)	Salt and brackish tidal shrub swamps
Estuarine Forested Wetland (E2FO)	Low-lying forests flooded periodically by tidal saltwater
Estuarine Unconsolidated Shore (E2US)	Periodically exposed salt and brackish tidal flats, bars, and beaches
Palustrine Forested Wetland (PFO)	Freshwater (tidal and nontidal) wooded swamps and bottomland hardwood wetlands
Palustrine Scrub-Shrub Wetland (PSS)	Freshwater (tidal and nontidal) shrub swamps and bogs
Palustrine Emergent Wetland (PEM)	Freshwater (tidal and nontidal) marshes and wet meadows
Palustrine Unconsolidated Shore (PUS)	Exposed, nonvegetated shorelines of ponds
Palustrine Unconsolidated Bottom (PUB)	Small ponds (open waterbodies generally less than 20 acres in size)
Palustrine Farmed Wetland (Pf)	Wetlands subject to prolonged seasonal inundation that are cultivated (they represent only the wettest depressions of farmfields where significant flooding was observed)
Lacustrine Habitats (L)	Freshwater lakes, reservoirs, and large, deep ponds (open waterbodies generally 20 acres or larger)
Riverine Habitats (R)	Freshwater rivers, streams, and creeks (tidal or nontidal)
Upland Agriculture (Ag L)	Cropland and pastures, including cultivated lands producing food for wildlife (e.g., regulated shooting areas in Maryland)
Urban Land (Urb L)	Built-up areas (with high density developments)
Rural Development (RDL)	Built-up areas outside of urban areas, with less than 50 people per square mile
Other Upland (Other L)	Uplands not falling in above categories (e.g., mining operations and forests)

Modifiers:
d	=	ditched, partially drained (applied to palustrine vegetated wetlands)
b	=	beaver-influenced (applied to palustrine wetlands)
th	=	timber-harvested (applied to forested wetlands that were logged during the study period and are now in a state of succession; does not include areas logged and now used for another purpose, such as a housing development or cropland).

equipment. Wetland status and trends data recorded on an overlay for each plot were scan-digitized for computer analysis.

Data Compilation and Analysis

Study data were compiled by computer using essentially the same program used to compile the national wetland trends study (Frayer, et al. 1983; Dahl and Johnson 1991). From a total of 760 sample plots, estimates of wetland acreages and of corresponding changes (between 1982 and 1989) were generated. For analysis, data were first compiled by individual wetland type at the class level within each system: estuarine emergent, scrub-shrub, forested, unconsolidated shore wetlands and palustrine forested, scrub-shrub, emergent, unconsolidated shore, and unconsolidated bottom wetlands.

For additional analysis, wetland classes were aggregated into vegetated and nonvegetated types by system: estuarine vegetated, palustrine vegetated, and estuarine nonvegetated, and palustrine nonvegetated (Table 5). These aggregations often improved the reliability of the estimated acreage and change acreages; due to larger estimates which usually tend to reduce variance.

Data for different types of palustrine wetlands were analyzed for assessing the impacts of timber harvest, ditching, and beaver. These findings are discussed in the text and presented in summary tables.

The effects of certain causes of wetland loss (destruction) or gain were determined as follows. The impact of factors responsible for wetland loss were calculated from their effect on the conversion of wetlands that existed in 1982. The following activities represented causes of wetland loss or destruction: excavation (e.g., channelization and marinas), pond and reservoir/lake construction, agricultural uses (including farmed wetlands), urban and rural development, and other development (e.g., sand and gravel mining and projects of unknown intent). Similarly, for determining the cause of a net gain in acreage of a particular wetland type (e.g., palustrine unconsolidated bottom), only the causes for the increased acreage were considered.

13

Table 5. Interpreted study categories and their aggregates used for data analysis. <u>Note</u>: In analyzing the data, several individual categories were combined into more generalized aggregated categories.

Interpreted Categories	Class Level Aggregates	Aggregated by Vegetation
Estuarine Subtidal Habitat (Deepwater Habitat)	Estuarine Subtidal	Estuarine Subtidal
Estuarine Emergent Wetland	Estuarine Emergent	Estuarine Vegetated
Estuarine Scrub-Shrub Wetland	Estuarine Scrub-Shrub	Estuarine Vegetated
Estuarine Forested Wetland	Estuarine Forested	Estuarine Vegetated
Estuarine Forested Wetland (Timber Harvested)*	Estuarine Forested	Estuarine Vegetated
Estuarine Unconsolidated Shore	Estuarine Unconsolidated Shore	Estuarine Nonvegetated
Palustrine Forested Wetland	Palustrine Forested	Palustrine Vegetated
Palustrine Forested/Ditched	Palustrine Forested	Palustrine Vegetated
Palustrine Forested/Beaver-modified	Palustrine Forested	Palustrine Vegetated
Palustrine Forested Wetland/Timber Harvested*	Palustrine Forested	Palustrine Vegetated
Palustrine Scrub-Shrub Wetland	Palustrine Scrub-Shrub	Palustrine Vegetated
Palustrine Scrub-Shrub/Ditched	Palustrine Scrub-Shrub	Palustrine Vegetated
Palustrine Scrub-Shrub/Beaver-modified	Palustrine Scrub-Shrub	Palustrine Vegetated
Palustrine Emergent Wetland	Palustrine Emergent	Palustrine Vegetated
Palustrine Emergent Wetland/Ditched	Palustrine Emergent	Palustrine Vegetated
Palustrine Emergent Wetland/Beaver-modified	Palustrine Emergent	Palustrine Vegetated
Palustrine Farmed Wetland	Palustrine Farmed	Palustrine Vegetated
Palustrine Unconsolidated Shore	Palustrine Unconsolidated Shore	Palustrine Nonvegetated
Palustrine Unconsolidated Bottom (Pond)	Palustrine Unconsolidated Bottom	Palustrine Nonvegetated
Palustrine Unconsolidated Bottom/Beaver-modified)	Palustrine Unconsolidated Bottom	Palustrine Nonvegetated
Lacustrine Open Water (Lake/Reservoir; mostly Deepwater Habitat)	Lacustrine	Lacustrine
Riverine Open Water (mostly Deepwater Habitat)	Riverine	Riverine
Agricultural Land	Agricultural Land	Agricultural Land
Urban Land	Urban Land	Urban Land
Rural Development Land	Rural Development Land	Rural Development Land
Other Land (e.g., forests and other development)	Other Land	Other Land

*This category was used to identify wetlands where timber was harvested; it was therefore applied only to "original" forested wetlands that were logged during the study period.

INTERPRETATION OF RESULTS

Wetland Definition

As mentioned earlier, this study uses the FWS wetland definition published in its official wetland classification system (Cowardin, et al. 1979). This definition was developed mainly to provide the foundation for conducting an inventory of the Nation's wetlands. This technically based definition was authored by a team of scientists from the FWS, the U.S. Geological Survey, the National Oceanic and Atmospheric Administration, and the University of Rhode Island. The document received widespread peer review and public comment prior to its official adoption by the FWS in 1979. The FWS wetland definition is not a regulatory definition, although for vegetated wetlands, it is consistent in concept with the Federal regulatory definition used for implementing the Clean Water Act (Federal Interagency Committee for Wetland Delineation 1989). Although consistent with such definition, the designation and delineation of wetlands following the FWS definition and the Federal regulatory definition may vary depending on the procedures used to identify the latter in the field. In general, the vegetated wetlands identified in this study are equivalent to those identified using the 1989 Federal interagency wetland delineation manual (Federal Interagency Committee for Wetland Delineation 1989) which was developed as a technical standard for identifying and delineating vegetated wetlands. The manual was adopted by the U.S. Army Corps of Engineers (Corps) and the U.S. Environmental Protection Agency from January, 1989 to August, 1991 for determining the limits of Federal jurisdiction in wetlands subject to the Clean Water Act (Tiner 1993a). It is still being used in several states, including Pennsylvania, Vermont, New Hampshire, Maine, and New Jersey. (Note: Prior to 1989, each Corps district had its own method for identifying regulated wetlands; no national standard existed. The 1987 Corps manual was developed for use by Corps personnel, but its use was discretionary by the districts.)

In August 1991, for various reasons, Congress effectively required the Corps to abandon use of the 1989 manual, so the Corps then adopted its previous manual for identifying wetlands subject to the Clean Water Act (Environmental Laboratory 1987; Tiner 1993a). Its use by Corps districts is now mandatory. The 1987 Corps manual mixes wetland policy with technical considerations in contrast to the ecologically based 1989 interagency manual.

Use of the 1987 Corps manual can lead to significant differences in identifying the presence and limits of wetlands due to varied interpretations. Seasonally saturated forested wetlands are usually not recognized as regulated wetlands following this manual. Thus, they are not currently subject to regulation and are more likely to be converted to other uses, than "regulated wetlands."

When interpreting study results, one must understand that not all wetlands identified in the study are currently subject to Federal, state, or local wetland regulatory requirements. This is especially true for palustrine wetlands. In contrast, all estuarine vegetated wetlands are Federally regulated wetlands and, in most cases, also state regulated wetlands. Since all wetlands are not "regulated" wetlands, one must exercise a certain amount of caution in attempting to evaluate the effectiveness of existing programs to control uses of "regulated" wetlands. The study does provide a perspective on the changing status of the wetland resources in the Watershed and allows those interested in wetland conservation to assess the effectiveness of various regulatory programs at protecting or controlling alterations of these natural resources. Wetland resource managers must decide whether these changes are acceptable and in the public interest or whether new initiatives must be undertaken to reverse these trends. It must also be emphasized that the study findings cover the period 1982 to 1989 and that the impact of recent improvements in Federal and state regulations cannot be analyzed. Yet the findings can be used to evaluate the extent to which wetlands were regulated prior to 1989.

Reliability of the Estimates

Estimated totals and their corresponding standard errors were calculated for major wetland types and other study categories for 1982 and 1989 and for recent changes in each category. For each estimate presented in the tables, an indication of the standard error (SE) is given. Standard errors are grouped into three ranges: (1) SE equal to or less than 20 percent of the estimated mean; (2) SE is less than 50 percent, but greater than 20 percent of the mean, and (3) SE is 50 percent of the mean or greater. Estimates cited in the text will also include their SE expressed as a percentage of the estimated total (%SE).

The estimates in this report vary in reliability. Many are highly reliable, but some others are not considered reliable enough to recommend their use for making decisions. An indication of reliability is given a measure called the sampling error percent. Sampling error percent is the standard error of an entry expressed as a percentage of the entry. Reliability can be stated generally as "we are 68 percent confident that the true value is within the interval constructed by adding to and subtracting from the entry the %SE/100 times the entry." For example, if an entry is 100 thousand acres and the %SE is 10, then we are 68 percent confident that the true value is between 90 thousand and 110 thousand acres. An equivalent statement for 95 percent confidence can be made by adding and subtracting twice the amount to and from the entry.

It is easy to see that a large %SE indicates low reliability, if any, in the estimate. In fact, if the %SE is 100 or greater, we cannot even say that we are 68 percent confident that the true value is not zero. In general, when the standard error is 20 percent or less of the estimated number, the estimate is considered reliable. The lower the %SE, the higher the reliability of the estimate and vice versa. If the %SE is 50 or more, one cannot even be 95 percent confident that the true value is not zero.

Generally, the estimates of trends will have higher sampling errors than the estimates of current quantities. This is because wetland trends are both positive and negative. In many cases, the resulting estimate of net change may be very close to zero. Such estimates often have high sampling errors even though the sampling design used (paired measurements or complete remeasurement) is the most precise design for measuring trends. In some cases, such as lakes and reservoirs (lacustrine open water), a high %SE indicates that the particular type is not as evenly distributed across the surface area as types with lower %SEs. High standard errors are also expected for many change categories where significant gains and losses are occurring simultaneously for a given wetland type. This situation simply reflects high variance which may be characteristic of the category estimated. Most change categories had this characteristic.

This discussion on reliability is meant to aid in interpretation of the study results. It was expected that only certain estimates would be precise enough to be meaningful. However, additional entries are included in the summary tables for additivity and ease of comparison.

Throughout this report, reference is made to acreages of wetland types and acreages of losses and gains. **The reader is cautioned that these numbers are estimates based on statistical sampling. These acreages, however, represent the best estimates to date on recent wetland status and trends for the Chesapeake Watershed available for evaluating wetland policies and to help formulate new protection strategies.** As noted above, standard errors of the estimates have been provided for those readers interested in the statistical reliability of the estimates. Readers should also be aware that acreage estimates reported in the text may, in limited cases, vary slightly when compared with numbers in the tables. This is due to computer round-off when combining categories in various ways for analysis. Although an effort was made to adjust the numbers, some estimates will not match. This difference, however, is not significant for interpreting study findings.

What is a Wetland Loss or Gain?

The answer to this question may seem obvious and trivial, but it is not. The results of a wetland trends study are usually reported as net losses or net gains in a given wetland type. These trends involve numerous interactions among existing wetlands, and between wetlands and uplands. These actions affect the 1989 acreage of a given wetland type, as demonstrated by the example for estuarine emergent wetlands (E2EM) given above. Net acreage changes result from: (1) conversions to nonwetlands (e.g., due to agriculture and urban development) and waterbodies which represent destroyed vegetated wetlands, (2) "losses" of a particular type related to changes to other vegetated wetland types (e.g., due to natural succession or human disturbance such as timber harvest of palustrine forests), and (3) increased acreage from wetland creation or natural succession from another wetland type (e.g., emergent wetland establishing in the shallow water zone of ponds). When the final tabulations are recorded, all the losses and the gains in individual areas are combined, with the final result being either a net gain or a net loss in that particular wetland type. So, all wetland types experience gains and losses with the net result being whatever amounts to the greatest acreage.

In this report, we have separated losses that represent destroyed wetlands from "losses" that are simply a change in vegetated wetland types (e.g., due to natural succession or timber harvest). Changes in vegetated wetlands that were considered true losses included the following actions: excavation (e.g., channelization and marinas), pond and reservoir/lake construction, agricultural uses (including farmed wetlands), urban and rural development, and other development (e.g., sand and gravel mining and projects of unknown purpose). These activities essentially eliminate most, if not all, wetland functions.

RESULTS FOR THE WATERSHED

Wetland Status

An estimated 5.2 million acres of wetlands and deepwater habitats existed in the Chesapeake Watershed in 1989. Wetlands alone accounted for almost 1.7 million acres. The Chesapeake's wetlands, therefore, cover an area about 1.4 times the size of Delaware or one-quarter of the size of Maryland. Nearly 4 percent of the 63,000-square mile Watershed was represented by wetlands. Palustrine wetlands (e.g., freshwater marshes, wet meadows, shrub swamps, wooded swamps, pine flatwoods, and bogs) were the most abundant, occupying about 1.46 million acres in the Watershed, while estuarine wetlands (e.g., salt and brackish marshes and forests) made up the remainder (about 205,000 acres) (Figures 3 and 4). Palustrine wetlands encompass an area about equal to the Western Shore of Maryland from Baltimore and Washington South. Estuarine wetlands cover an area about five times the size of the District of Columbia or four times the size of Baltimore. Palustrine forested wetlands were the most common type (about 990,000 acres), representing about 60 percent of the Watershed's wetlands. Palustrine scrub-shrub wetlands (roughly 177,000 acres) were next in abundance, followed closely by estuarine emergent wetlands (about 170,000 acres) and palustrine emergent wetlands (roughly 167,000 acres). About 115,000 acres of ponds occurred in the Watershed.

The Chesapeake Watershed includes nearly 3.5 million acres of deepwater habitats (e.g., estuaries, lakes, reservoirs, and rivers). Almost 80 percent of this total is represented by estuarine waters - Chesapeake Bay and its tributaries (2,782,219 acres, 1.6% SE). Lakes and reservoirs make up 13 percent of the total (469,822 acres, 36.3% SE), while rivers comprise the remaining 7 percent (244,580 acres, 28.9% SE).

About 40 percent of the Chesapeake Watershed wetlands occur in Virginia which has almost 670,000 acres, mostly palustrine forested wetlands (Figure 5; Tables 6 and 7). Maryland has over 25 percent of the Watershed's wetlands, while Pennsylvania and New York are the only other states having more than 10 percent of the basin's wetlands. Acreage totals by state for each wetland type are summarized in Table 6, with percentages of estuarine and palustrine wetlands in the Chesapeake Watershed given by state in Table 7.

Figure 3. Estimated 1989 wetland acreages for the Chesapeake Watershed.

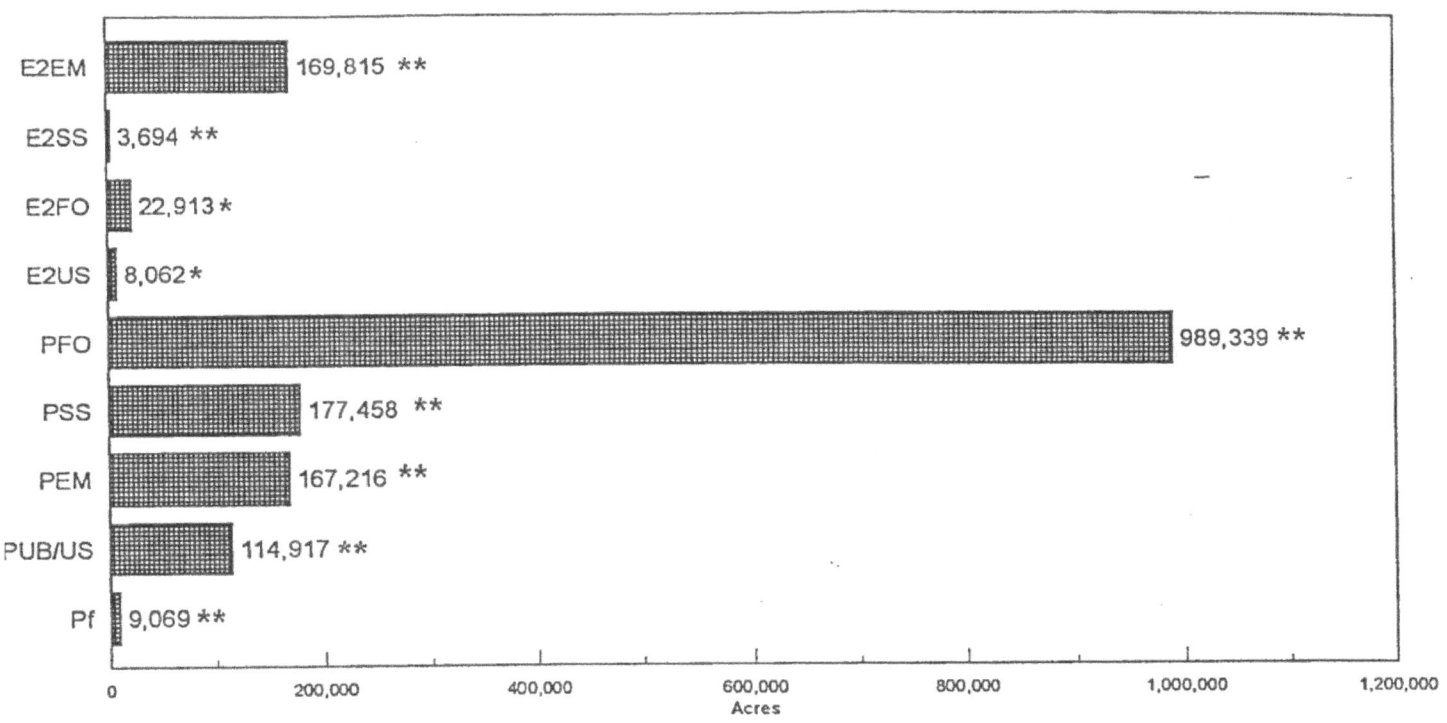

E2EM — 169,815 **
E2SS — 3,694 **
E2FO — 22,913 *
E2US — 8,062 *
PFO — 989,339 **
PSS — 177,458 **
PEM — 167,216 **
PUB/US — 114,917 **
Pf — 9,069 **

**Standard error is 20% or less of the estimate.
*Standard error is between 20 - 50% of the estimate.

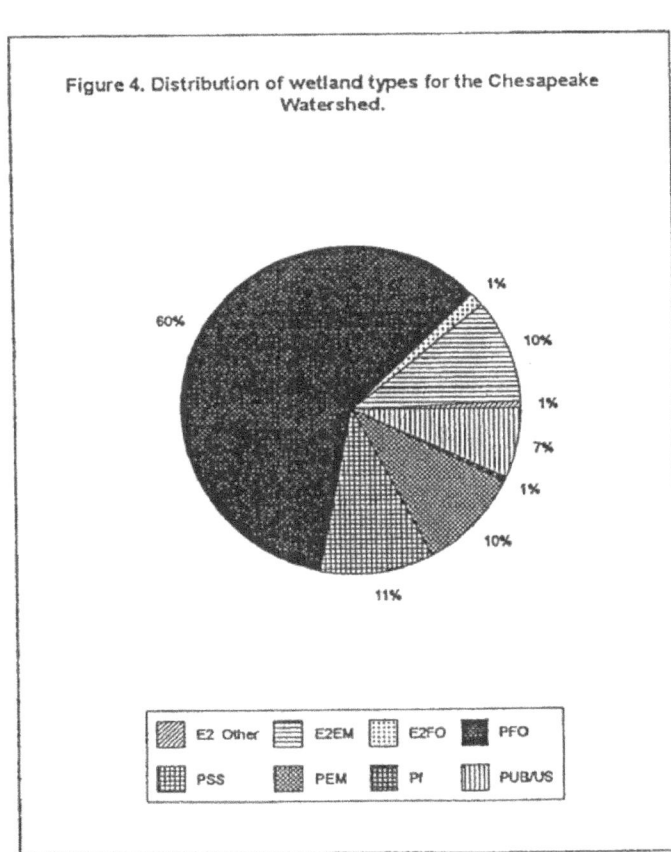

Figure 4. Distribution of wetland types for the Chesapeake Watershed.

1%
10%
1%
7%
1%
10%
11%
60%

E2 Other   E2EM   E2FO   PFO
PSS   PEM   Pf   PUB/US

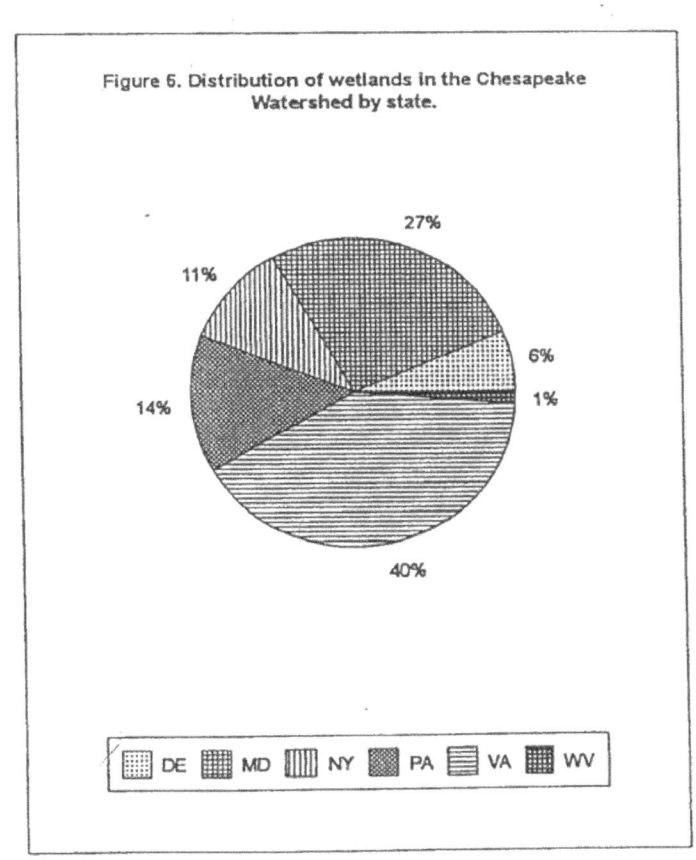

Figure 5. Distribution of wetlands in the Chesapeake Watershed by state.

27%
11%
6%
1%
14%
40%

DE   MD   NY   PA   VA   WV

Table 6. Estimated 1989 wetland acreages in the Chesapeake Watershed by state.

Wetland Type	DE Acreage	MD Acreage	NY Acreage	PA Acreage	VA Acreage	WV Acreage
					—	~
Estuarine Wetlands						
Emergent	---	96,453**	---	---	73,362**	---
Scrub-Shrub	---	2,396*	---	---	1,298*	---
Forested	---	18,227*	---	---	4,686	---
Unconsolidated Shore	---	2,933*	---	---	5,129*	---
Total	---	120,009**	---	---	84,475**	---
Palustrine Wetlands						
Forested	91,407**	262,128**	77,737	120,100**	430,013**	7,954*
Scrub-Shrub	5,580**	20,852**	45,594	46,050*	57,782**	1,600
Emergent	2,189*	20,243**	40,649*	42,459*	53,226**	8,450
Unconsolidated Shore	43	502*	---	955*	363*	---
Unconsolidated Bottom	1,108**	17,777**	17,110	30,574**	42,500**	3,985*
Farmed	4,564*	2,542*	---	131	1,640	192
Total	104,891**	324,044**	181,090	240,269**	585,524**	22,181*
Total Wetlands	104,891**	444,053**	181,090	240,269**	669,999**	22,181*

**   Standard error is equal to or less than 20 percent of the estimated acreage.

*   Standard error is less than 50 percent of the estimate, but greater than 20 percent of the estimated acreage.

Note: Estimates without an asterisk have higher standard errors.

Table 7. Percent of Chesapeake Watershed wetlands in each state.

State	% of Estuarine Wetlands	% of Palustrine Wetlands	% of Total Watershed Wetlands
Delaware	—	7.2	6.3
Maryland	59	22.2	26.7
New York	—	12.4	10.9
Pennsylvania	—	16.5	14.5
Virginia	41	40.2	40.3
West Virginia	—	1.5	1.3

Status of Estuarine Wetlands

Of the nearly 205,000 acres of estuarine wetlands (196,422 vegetated acres, 12.6% SE; 8,062 nonvegetated acres, 27.7% SE) that were present in the Chesapeake Watershed in 1989, 83 percent were marshes dominated by halophytic (salt-tolerant) grasses and grasslike plants (169,815 acres, 12.2% SE)(Figures 3 and 6). Eleven percent of the estuarine wetlands were forests (22,913 acres, 35.8% SE), mostly low-lying loblolly pine (Pinus taeda) flatwoods, that are now irregularly flooded by the tides. This condition is most likely due to sea level rise and coastal subsidence and enhanced by local ditching. Flooding by saltwater stresses these forests, leading to chlorosis (yellowing of pine needles), colonization of herb stratum by halophytes, and when severe, eventually leads to the death of the pines and replacement of the forest with salt marsh. This is a natural process called salt marsh transgression where salt marshes are moving landward in response to rising sea level and coastal subsidence. Figure 6 shows the percent breakdown for all estuarine wetland types.

About 59 percent of the Bay's estuarine wetlands are found in Maryland: 117,076 vegetated acres (16.9% SE) and 2,933 nonvegetated acres (37.4% SE). The remaining 41 percent occurs in Virginia: 79,346 vegetated acres (18.7% SE) and 5,129 nonvegetated acres (37.9% SE). Table 6 provides further breakdowns of the estuarine wetland totals by wetland type.

Status of Palustrine Wetlands

Of the nearly 1.5 million acres of palustrine wetlands (1,343,082 vegetated acres, 8.5% SE; 114,917 nonvegetated acres, 10.3% SE) in the Watershed, about 68 percent are forested wetlands (989,339 acres, 8.0% SE) (Figures 3 and 7). Scrub-shrub wetlands and emergent wetlands (marshes and wet meadows) account for 12 and 11 percent of the Watershed's freshwater wetlands (177,458 acres, 16.4% SE; 167,216 acres, 12.1% SE), respectively. Ponds represent nearly 8 percent of the Watershed's palustrine wetlands (114,917 acres, 10.3% SE). Figure 7 shows the percent breakdown for all palustrine wetland types.

Thirty-eight percent of the Watershed's palustrine wetlands occur within the Coastal Flats region. The remaining palustrine wetlands fall equally within the Rolling Plains and Appalachian Highlands strata (31 percent each).

Roughly 40 percent of the Watershed's palustrine wetlands are located in Virginia (Table 7). Maryland possesses 22 percent of these wetlands, while Pennsylvania accounts for over 16 percent.

Wetland Density

Wetland densities and percent of land covered by wetlands for all strata, except the Coastal Zone (which is nearly exclusively estuarine wetland and deepwater habitat associated with Chesapeake Bay and its tidal tributaries) are presented in Table 8. Wetland density was highest in the Pothole stratum of Delaware, with about 173 wetland acres per square mile (27 percent of the surface area). The Pothole stratum is part of the Coastal Flats region which averaged 95 wetland acres per square mile (nearly 15 percent of the surface area). The lowest wetland density in the Watershed was found in the Virginia portion of the Appalachian Highlands with only 3 wetland acres per square mile. Overall, the Appalachian Highlands region averaged about 12 acres per square mile which represents slightly less than 2 percent of the land surface. Wetland density increased substantially in the recently glaciated section of this province to about 17 to 40 wetland acres per square mile, well above the coverage in the nonglaciated section of the Appalachian Highlands.

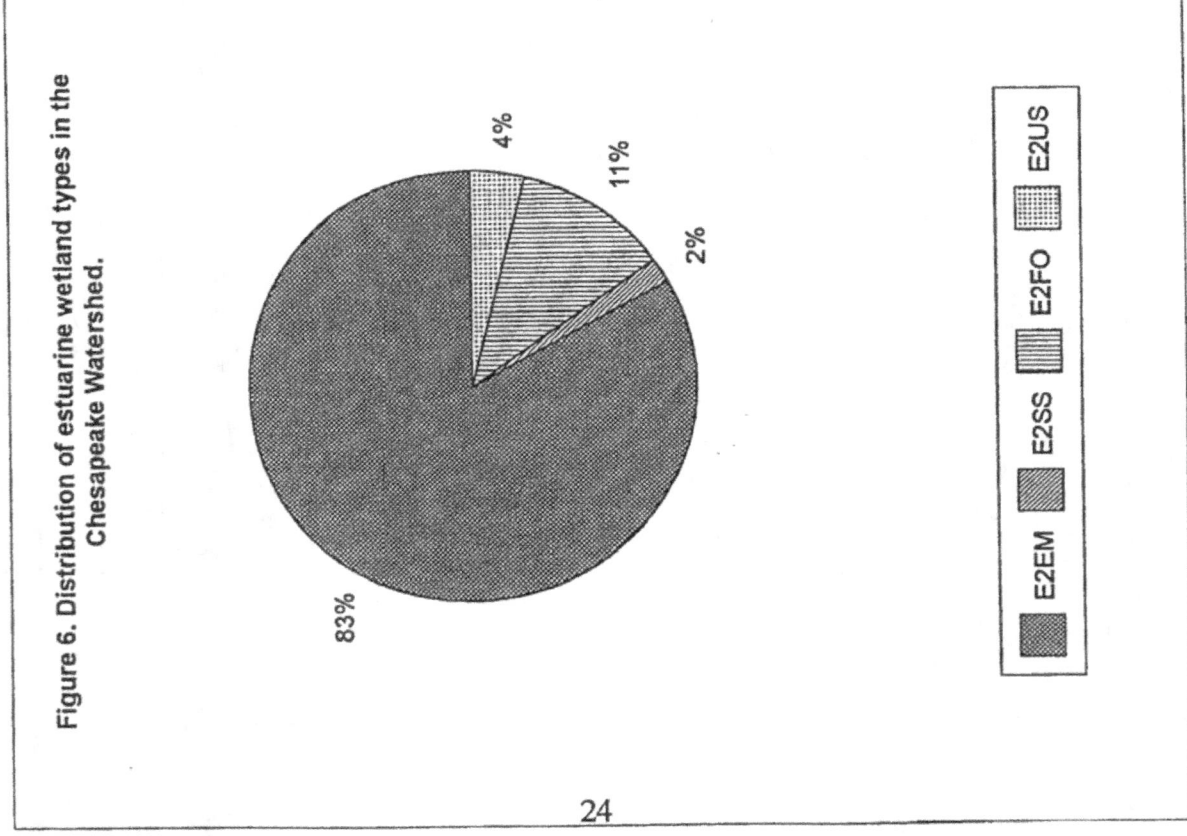

Figure 7. Distribution of palustrine wetland types in the Chesapeake Watershed.

1%

8%

11%

12%

68%

PFO

PSS

PEM

PUB/US

Pf

Figure 6. Distribution of estuarine wetland types in the Chesapeake Watershed.

4%

11%

2%

83%

E2EM

E2SS

E2FO

E2US

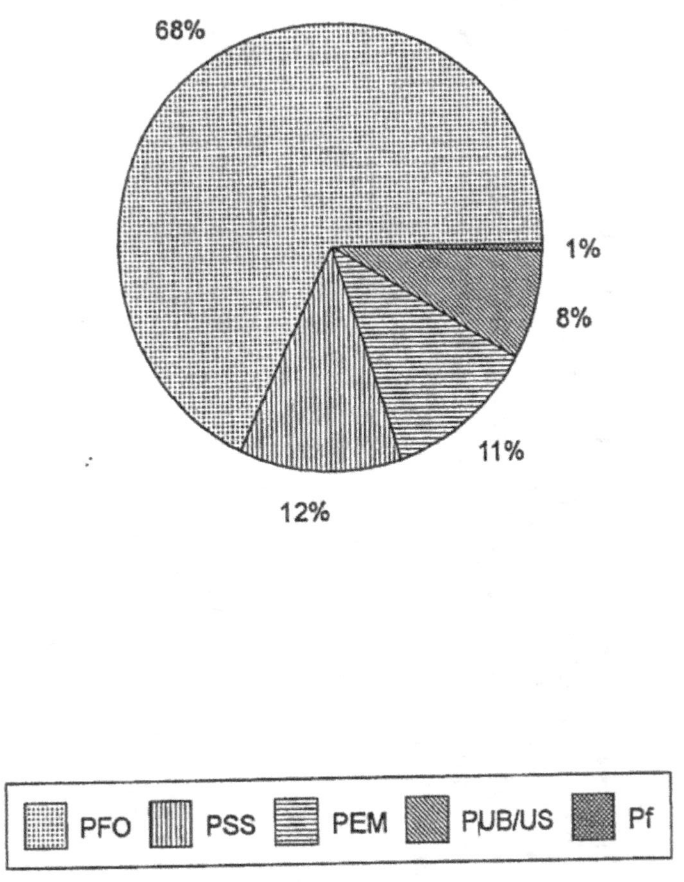

Table 8. Wetland densities and percent of the land surface covered by wetlands for sampling strata within the Chesapeake Watershed for 1989.

Stratum	State	Wetland Density (Acres/Sq. Mi.)	% of Surface Area Covered by Wetland
COASTAL FLATS			—
Pothole Region	DE	172.7	27.0
	MD	134.2	21.0
(Subtotal Potholes)		(145.5)	(22.7)
Southeast Metro	VA	72.1	11.3
Rest of Coastal Flats	DE	138.5	21.6
	MD	67.5	10.5
	VA	112.2	17.5
(Subtotal Rest of Coastal Flats)		(90.6)	(14.2)
TOTAL COASTAL FLATS		95.1	14.9
ROLLING PLAIN			
Rolling Plains #2	MD	18.2	2.8
	VA	46.3	7.2
Rolling Plain #1	MD	14.9	2.3
	PA	7.1	1.1
	VA	24.2	3.8
TOTAL ROLLING PLAINS		23.7	3.7
APPALACHIAN HIGHLANDS			
Poconos 1*	PA	40.3	6.3
Poconos 2*	PA	24.7	3.9
Other Glaciated*	PA	16.9	2.6
Rest of Appalachian Highlands	PA	9.6	1.5
Appalachian Highlands	MD	5.0	0.8
	NY*	29.3	4.6
	VA	3.0	0.5
	WV	6.2	1.0
TOTAL APPALACHIAN HIGHLANDS		11.8	1.9
WATERSHED GRAND TOTAL		23.1	3.6

*Recently Glaciated - Wisconsin glaciation, roughly 10-12,000 years B.P.

Ditched Palustrine Wetlands[1]

Ditching of palustrine vegetated wetlands has been quite extensive in the Chesapeake Watershed. Ditching impairs the natural functions of wetlands to some extent. Nearly 100,000 acres of these wetlands are ditched (Table 9), amounting to 7.2 percent of the Watershed's palustrine vegetated wetlands. Forested wetlands were most heavily ditehed, with 83,341 acres (17.2% SE) partly drained. This represents 8 percent of the Watershed's palustrine forests.

Ditching was most prevalent in Coastal Plain wetlands (Coastal Flats and Pothole Region strata). Surprisingly, almost half of the ditched forested wetlands in the Watershed occur in the Delaware portion of the Watershed: 41,458 acres (25.1% SE). This is quite impressive, considering that this area comprises only 1 percent of the Watershed. Also surprising was the ditching of over 7,748 acres (61.2% SE) of forested wetlands in the Southeast Metro region of Virginia. This figure represents 9 percent of the ditched forested wetlands in the Watershed, yet the region also represents only 1 percent of the Watershed's land area. Ditched scrub-shrub and emergent wetlands were nearly equal in abundance in 1989, with 7,169 acres (41.0% SE) and 6,134 acres (49.4% SE), respectively.

---

[1]Ditched wetlands are defined as wetlands partly drained by open ditches, but still retaining sufficient wetness to be considered wetlands. Effectively drained former wetlands are not included in this discussion, since they are not classified as "wetland" because they no longer have wetland hydrologic conditions.

Table 9. Estimated acreage of ditched palustrine wetlands in the Chesapeake Watershed in 1989. (Note: State and Watershed totals may be slightly different than the sum of individual strata due to round-off.)

State	Stratum	PFO Acres	PSS Acres	PEM Acres
Delaware	Potholes	12,475*	118	37
	Rest of Coastal Flats	28,983*	2,047*	476
	(STATE TOTAL)	(41,458*)	(2,165*)	(513)
Maryland	Coastal Zone	714	—	—
	Potholes	11,693*	561	541
	Rest of Coastal Flats	9,775*	734	231*
	Rolling Plain #2	—	—	122
	Appalachian Highlands	—	109	—
	(STATE TOTAL)	(22,182**)	(1,404*)	(894*)
Pennsylvania	Rolling Plain	—	—	43
	Poconos #2	—	—	5
	Rest of Appalachian Highlands	—	—	275
	(STATE TOTAL)	—	—	323
Virginia	Coastal Zone	1,550	132	466
	Southeast Metro	7,748	112	24
	Rest of Coastal Flats	10,033	3,153	3,548
	Rolling Plain #1	—	203	203
	Rolling Plain #2	370	—	35
	(STATE TOTAL)	(19,701*)	(3,600)	(4,276)
West Virginia	Appalachian Highlands	—	—	128
WATERSHED	**ALL STRATA**	83,341**	7,169*	6,134*

** Standard error is 20 percent or less than the estimate.

* Standard error is less than 50 percent of the estimate, but greater than 20 percent of the estimate.

Note: Estimates without an asterisk have higher standard errors.

Beaver-modified Wetlands

Beaver activity in wetlands was detected in all physiographic regions in the Watershed, with nearly 100,000 acres affected (Table 10). Sixty-nine percent of these wetlands were in Virginia's Rolling Plain, mostly in the Piedmont province (Rolling Plain #1). Pennsylvania's wetlands also had a substantial amount of beaver influence, accounting for about 27 percent of the Watershed's beaver activity in the Chesapeake Watershed.

Table 10. Estimated acreage of beaver-modified wetlands in the Chesapeake Watershed in 1989. (Note: State and Watershed totals may vary slightly from the sum of individual strata due to round-off.)

State	Stratum	PFO Acres	PSS Acres	PEM Acres	PUB Acres
Maryland	Coastal Zone	---	26	---	---
	Coastal Flats	63	15	92	41
	Irregular Plain	117	---	---	82
	Appalachian Highland	104	89	533	212
	(MD TOTAL)	(284)	(130)	(625)	(335)
Pennsylvania	Poconos #1	2	34*	81*	17*
	Poconos #2	145*	155*	483*	174
	Other Glaciated	938*	2,719*	1,935*	534
	Rest of Appalachian Highlands	3,783	8,322	5,685	711
	(PA TOTAL)	(4,868)	(11,230)	(8,184**)	(1,436**)
Virginia	Southeast Metro	107	20	---	82
	Rest of Coastal Flats	884*	757	181*	407
	Rolling Plain #2	8,819**	7,144*	3,404*	1,799*
	Rolling Plain #1	24,952	11,357*	5,006*	2,910*
	Appalachian Highlands	53	---	---	---
	(VA TOTAL)	(34,815*)	(19,278*)	(8,591*)	(5,198*)
West Virginia	Appalachian Highlands	176	---	---	---
Watershed	**ALL STRATA**	**40,143***	**30,638***	**17,400***	**6,969****

** Standard error estimate is equal to or less than 20 percent of the estimated acreage.

* Standard error is less than 50 percent of the estimate, but greater than 20 percent of the estimated acreage.

Note: Estimates without an asterisk have higher standard errors.

Recent Trends in Estuarine Wetlands

Estuarine vegetated wetlands had a net loss of 904 acres (52.7% SE) from 197,326 acres (12.6% SE) in 1982 to 196,422 acres (12.6% SE) in 1989. This amounts to a net loss of about 0.5 percent of the Chesapeake Bay's estuarine vegetated wetlands. An estimated 1,145 acres (26.5% SE) were destroyed (converted to nonwetland or open water). This loss was largely due to impoundment construction and human-induced alterations changing these wetlands to nonwetlands. Rising sea level combined with coastal erosion and dredging activities also affected significant acreage. An estimated 400 acres (64.3% SE) of these wetlands were diked to create freshwater wetlands (including farmed wetlands), with an additional 70 acres (64.3% SE) converted to freshwater impoundments. Coastal erosion, sea level rise, and dredging projects changed 296 acres (26.7% SE) to estuarine deepwater habitats. About 668 acres (36.5% SE) were converted to agricultural land (including farmed wetlands) and filled for various development projects in urban and rural areas. An estimated total of 298 acres (48.7% SE) of estuarine vegetated wetlands were converted to upland agriculture. This includes diking marshes and producing crops such as milo for wildlife at regulated shooting areas. Besides the destroyed wetlands, 387 acres (66.6% SE) changed to palustrine vegetated wetlands, and 403 acres (54.0% SE) of new estuarine vegetated wetlands came from palustrine vegetated wetlands and another 225 acres (39.4% SE) from other habitats.

Figure 8 identifies causes of estuarine emergent wetland losses. Thirty-eight percent of the losses involved converting marshes to open water. Multiple factors are responsible for this, including coastal erosion, dredging, rising sea level, and coastal subsidence. Agriculture (including cropland associated with regulated shooting areas) accounted for a surprising 24 percent change.

Maryland had the greatest decline of estuarine forested wetlands, while Virginia had the greatest losses of emergent wetlands and unconsolidated shores (tidal flats). The latter type increased in acreage in Maryland during the study area. In both states, estuarine scrub-shrub wetlands increased slightly. (Refer to state summaries for details.)

Recent Trends in Palustrine Wetlands

Palustrine vegetated wetlands declined by almost 2 percent during the study period (from 1,353,664 acres, 8.3% SE in 1982 to 1,334,012 acres, 8.5% SE in 1989). An estimated total of 36,033 acres (38.8% SE) were destroyed during this 7-year period. These losses amount to an area about the size of the District of Columbia. An estimated 403 acres (54.0% SE) changed to estuarine vegetated wetlands. Increases in palustrine vegetated wetland acreage came from estuarine vegetated wetlands (387 acres, 66.6% SE) and ponds, lakes, uplands, and other habitats (16,397 acres, 33.9% SE). Lake/reservoir construction (14,543 acres, 95.1% SE), agriculture (11,513 acres, 18.5% SE) and pond construction (7,239 acres, 11.7% SE) were responsible for most (86 percent) of the losses of the original palustrine vegetated wetlands. Figures 9, 10, and 11 show the causes of wetland destruction for palustrine forested, scrub-shrub, and emergent wetlands, respectively.

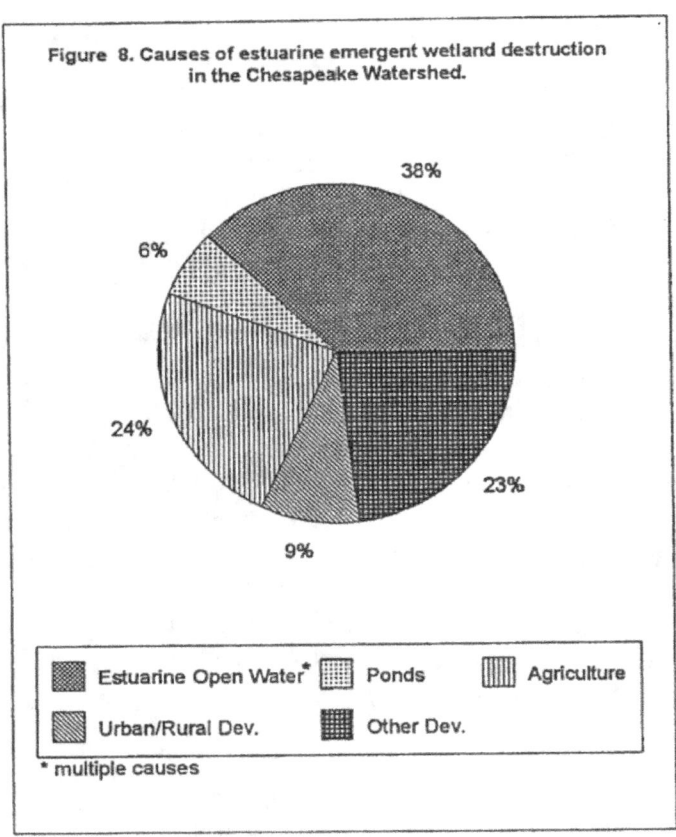

Figure 8. Causes of estuarine emergent wetland destruction in the Chesapeake Watershed.

38%
6%
24%
9%
23%

Estuarine Open Water*   Ponds   Agriculture
Urban/Rural Dev.   Other Dev.
* multiple causes

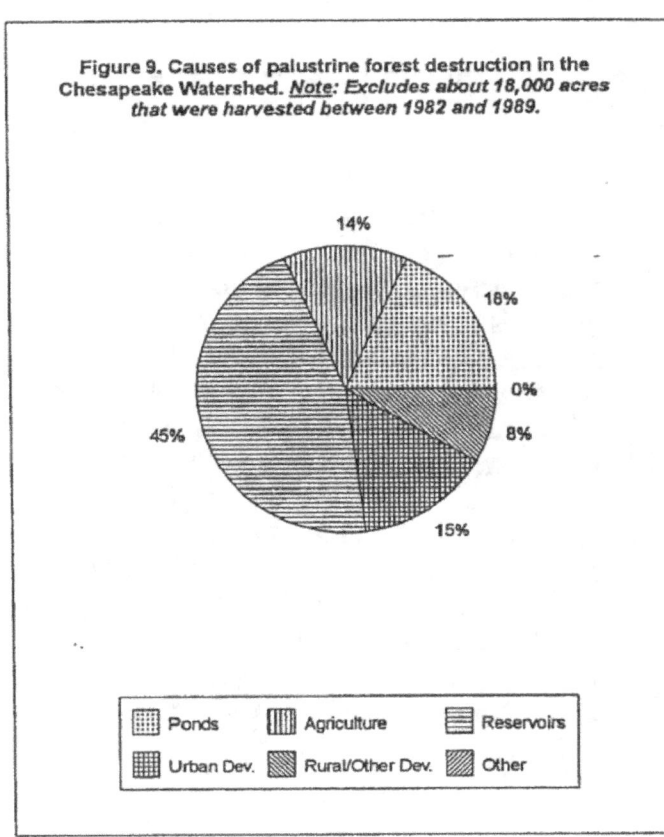

Figure 9. Causes of palustrine forest destruction in the Chesapeake Watershed. *Note: Excludes about 18,000 acres that were harvested between 1982 and 1989.*

14%
18%
0%
8%
15%
45%

Ponds   Agriculture   Reservoirs
Urban Dev.   Rural/Other Dev.   Other

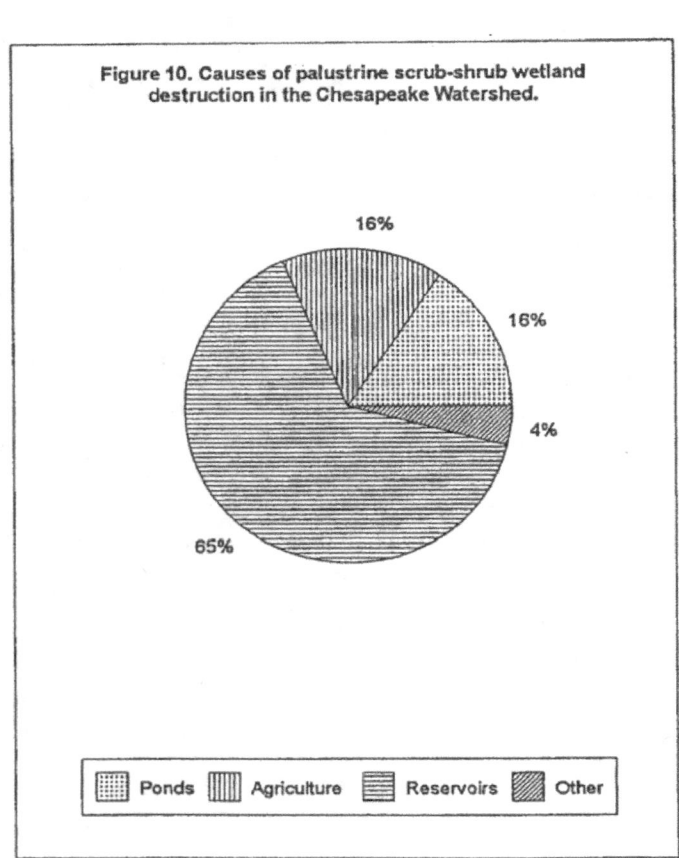

Figure 10. Causes of palustrine scrub-shrub wetland destruction in the Chesapeake Watershed.

16%
16%
4%
65%

Ponds   Agriculture   Reservoirs   Other

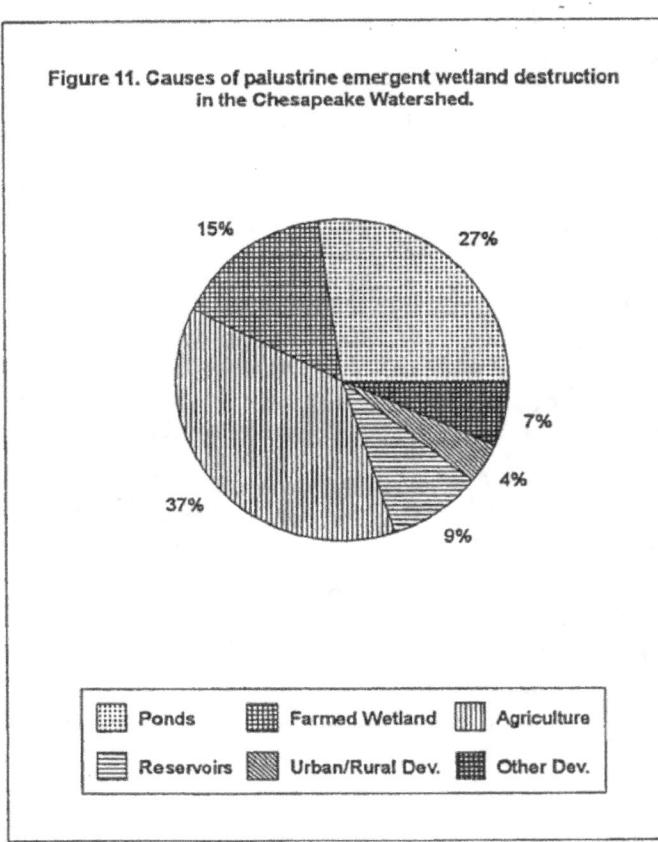

Figure 11. Causes of palustrine emergent wetland destruction in the Chesapeake Watershed.

15%
27%
7%
4%
9%
37%

Ponds   Farmed Wetland   Agriculture
Reservoirs   Urban/Rural Dev.   Other Dev.

Although palustrine forested wetlands alone experienced a net decline of 14,406 acres (41.5% SE), much of this "loss" was due to timber harvest operations. Of the 1,003,745 acres (7.9% SE) of palustrine forests that existed in 1982, nearly 2 percent (18,036 acres, 16.1% SE) was harvested between 1982 and 1989. These "losses" of palustrine forests actually accounted for some gains in other palustrine vegetated wetlands. For example, cutover loblolly pine (Pinus taeda) flatwoods often become wet meadows dominated by woolgrass (Scirpus cyperinus), which in time are replaced by scrub-shrub wetlands represented mainly by saplings of tree species. Eventually, palustrine forests are re-established. Much acreage of palustrine vegetated wetlands seems to be affected by forestry and is in a state of transition in the timber management cycle. Timber harvest of palustrine forested wetlands in the Watershed was largely concentrated in the Coastal Plain of the Watershed. From 1982 to 1989, Virginia had the highest acreage of harvested palustrine forests: 9,280 acres (20.8% SE). Maryland closely followed with 7,529 acres (27.8% SE). Delaware was the only other state where harvesting of palustrine forests was observed; it had 1,227 acres (49.2% SE) cut over during the study period. These changes were largely responsible for the "losses" of palustrine forests in Virginia, Maryland, and Delaware between 1982 and 1989.

Net increases in palustrine scrub-shrub wetlands were recorded in most states, except for Virginia and Pennsylvania where net losses of 8,042 acres (96.2% SE) and 920 acres (183.4% SE) were estimated, respectively. Maryland had the largest gain in scrub-shrub wetlands, mainly from: (1) cut-over palustrine forests and, (2) through succession from previous wet meadows which probably represent former forested wetlands that were harvested prior to 1982.

All states, except Pennsylvania, had net declines in the acreage of palustrine emergent wetlands. The largest net losses were in Virginia (-2,846 acres, 104.3% SE), with Delaware (-1,774 acres, 47.8% SE) and Maryland (-1,638 acres, 80.0% SE) also losing substantial amounts. Most of the palustrine emergent wetland changes in Virginia were to palustrine scrub-shrub wetlands (8,232 acres, 34.0% SE), agriculture (1,462 acres, 56.4% SE), pond construction (1,336 acres, 29.0% SE), and lake/reservoir construction (969 acres, 97.9% SE). Delaware lost 1,155 acres (49.3% SE) of emergent wetlands to farmed wetlands and another 534 acres (33.0% SE) to upland agriculture. Maryland also lost considerable acreage to farming activities, with 1,046 acres (24.6% SE) to upland agriculture and 439 acres (41.7% SE) to farmed wetlands. Surprisingly, Pennsylvania had a net increase of 3,055 acres (163.1% SE) in palustrine emergent wetland acreage. Most of the new acreage came from ponds (5,417 acres, 46.9% SE), lakes/reservoirs (2,401 acres, 94.9% SE), and palustrine scrub-shrub wetlands (1,689 acres, 48.7% SE). These and other gains when combined with losses of almost 7,800 acres of Pennsylvania's emergent wetlands present in 1982, produced the net gain of 3,055 acres (163.1% SE).

Palustrine nonvegetated wetlands (e.g., ponds) increased in acreage by 5,634 acres (55.4% SE). The new ponds came mostly from palustrine vegetated wetlands (7,239 acres, 11.7% SE), "other" upland (5,188 acres, 23.1% SE), and agricultural land (3,218 acres, 17.8% SE). Pond acreage increased mostly in Virginia and Maryland, with a considerable gain also in West Virginia. Other states, notably Pennsylvania, had net decreases in ponds. The gains in ponds in the Chesapeake Watershed came mainly from vegetated wetlands (about 7,000

31

acres), nonagricultural uplands (about 5,000 acres), and agricultural land (about 3,000 acres). The recent decline in open water pond acreage in Pennsylvania was mostly attributed to the establishment of palustrine emergent wetlands in ponds. Here 5,417 acres (46.9% SE) of the 1982 pond (open water) acreage changed to this wetland type, presumably due to sedimentation, while only 811 acres (29.6% SE) of the new ponds were excavated from emergent wetlands.

RESULTS BY STATE

Tables 11 and 12 summarize the wetland changes in the Chesapeake Bay Watershed by state. Table 13 reviews forestry (timber harvest) impacts. Following these tables are discussions of wetland status and recent trends for the portion of each state located in the Watershed.

Table 11. Changes in vegetated wetlands in the Chesapeake Watershed and in the portion of each state contained in the Watershed. (Watershed totals may differ slightly from the sum of state totals due to computer round-off.)

STATE	Vegetated Wetland Type	1982 Acres	1989 Acres	Acres Changed to Other Veg. Wetlands	Acres Gained From Other Veg. Wetlands	Acres Destroyed	Acres Gained From Other Habitats	Net Change
Delaware	Palustrine	102,103 **	99,176 **	—	—	3,207 *	281 *	-2,927 *
Maryland	Palustrine	307,546 **	303,223 **	397	315	5,358 **	1,115 *	-4,323 **
	Estuarine	117,635 **	117,076 **	315	397	733 *	92 *	-559
New York	Palustrine	163,881	163,980	—	—	0	99	+99
Pennsylvania	Palustrine	203,926 **	208,609 **	---	---	3,977 *	8,660	+4,683
Virginia	Palustrine	558,492 **	541,021 **	6	72	23,474	5,937 *	-17,471
	Estuarine	79,690 **	79,346 **	72	6	412 *	133	-344
West Virginia	Palustrine	17,716 *	18,004 *	---	---	16	304	+288
CHESAPEAKE WATERSHED	Palustrine	1,353,664 **	1,334,012 **	403	387	36,033 *	16,397 *	-19,652
	Estuarine	197,326 **	196,422 **	387	403	1,145 *	225 *	-904

**   Standard error is 20 percent or less than the estimate.

*   Standard error is less than 50 percent of the estimate, but greater than 20 percent of the estimate.

Note: Estimates without an asterisk have higher standard errors.

Table 12. Changes in specific types of vegetated wetlands in the Chesapeake Watershed (1982-1989).

Vegetated Wetland Type	1982 Acres	1989 Acres	Acres Changed to Other Veg Wetlands	Acres Gained From Veg Wetlands	Acres Destroyed	Acres Gained From Other Areas	Net Change
PFO	1,003,745 **	989,339 **	25,655 **	22,355 **	14,700 *	3,594	-14,406 *
PSS	178,424 **	177,458 **	26,673 **	35,193 **	10,693	1,207 *	-966
PEM	171,499 **	167,216 **	19,230 **	13,993 **	10,642 **	11,596 *	-4,283
E2EM	170,311 **	169,815 **	281 *	741	1,085 *	129 *	-496
E2SS	3,231 **	3,694 **	196 *	590 *	0	69	+463 *
E2FO	23,784 *	22,913 *	1,306	469 *	62	28	-871

**   Standard error is 20 percent or less than the estimate.

*   Standard error is less than 50 percent of the estimate, but greater than 20 percent of the estimate.

Note: Estimates without an asterisk have higher standard errors.

Table 13. Estimated acreage of palustrine forested wetlands that were harvested between 1982 and 1989 in the Chesapeake Watershed. (Note: State and Watershed totals may vary slightly from the sum of individual strata due to round-off.)

State	Stratum	Acres
Delaware	Coastal Flats	1,227 *
Maryland	Coastal Zone	1,916
	Potholes	249
	Rest of Coastal Flats	5,364 *
	(STATE TOTAL)	(7,529 *)
Virginia	Coastal Zone	1,073
	Southeast Metro	504 *
	Rest of Coastal Flats	5,231 *
	Rolling Plain #2 (Upper Coastal Plain)	2,425
	Rolling Plain #1 (Piedmont)	47
	(STATE TOTAL)	(9,280 **)
WATERSHED	**ALL STRATA**	18,036 **

**   Standard error is 20 percent or less of the estimate.

*   Standard error is less than 50 percent of the estimate, but greater than 20 percent of the estimate.

Note: Estimates without an asterisk have higher standard errors.

DELAWARE

Study findings for the Delaware portion of the Chesapeake Watershed are presented in Table 14, Figures 12-15, and in the following discussion. This 709-square mile area represents about 1 percent of the Watershed. It also represents about 37 percent of Delaware.

Current Status

Wetlands occupy about 105,000 acres in the Delaware portion of the Chesapeake Watershed. This averages about 23 percent of the land surface and equates to an area about one-quarter the size of Kent County. The Pothole region had 172.7 wetland acres/square mile (27% of the area), while the rest of the area had 138.5 wetland acres/square mile (22% of the area). Palustrine forests were the predominant type, with 91,407 acres (13.5% SE). Figures 12 and 13 show the acreages and percentages of each type of palustrine wetland. Forty-five percent of the forested wetlands are affected by ditching and channelization (41,458 acres, 25.0% SE) (Table 9). This portion of Delaware had about 46 percent of the ditched wetlands in the entire Chesapeake Watershed. Given that this area represents only 1 percent of the Watershed's area, the effect of ditching here is disproportional to its area.

Recent Trends

From 1982 to 1989, palustrine vegetated wetlands decreased by a net total of 2,926 acres (28.6% SE). This figure represents a nearly 3 percent loss in just 7 years. Actually, more than 3,000 acres of these wetlands were destroyed (Table 14). The causes of palustrine forest destruction were agriculture (61%, including farmed wetlands), unspecified development (24%), urban and rural development (9%), and pond/impoundment construction (6%) (Figure 14). In addition, about 1,200 acres of palustrine forests were harvested between 1982 and 1989, but this action represents a change in wetland type. Almost 2,000 acres of palustrine emergent wetlands were converted to dryland or waterbodies during the study period. This amounts to half of the freshwater marshes and meadows that existed in this area in 1982. The causes for palustrine emergent wetland destruction were agriculture (87%, with most of the acreage converted to farmed wetland), unspecified development (10%), and pond construction (3%) (Figure 15).

36

Table 14. Changes in specific types of vegetated wetlands in the Delaware portion of the Chesapeake Watershed (1982-1989).

Vegetated Wetland Type	1982 Acres	1989 Acres	Acres Changed to Other Veg Wetlands	Acres Gained From Veg Wetlands	Acres Destroyed	Acres Gained-From Other Areas	Net Change
PFO	94,205 **	91,407 **	2,268 *	579 *	1,109 *	0	-2,798 **
PSS	3,935 *	5,580 **	767 *	2,452 *	151 *	111	+1,645 *
PEM	3,963 *	2,189 *	624	627	1,947 *	170 *	-1,774 *

**   Standard error is 20 percent or less than the estimate.

*   Standard error is less than 50 percent of the estimate, but greater than 20 percent of the estimate.

Note: Estimates without an asterisk have higher standard errors.

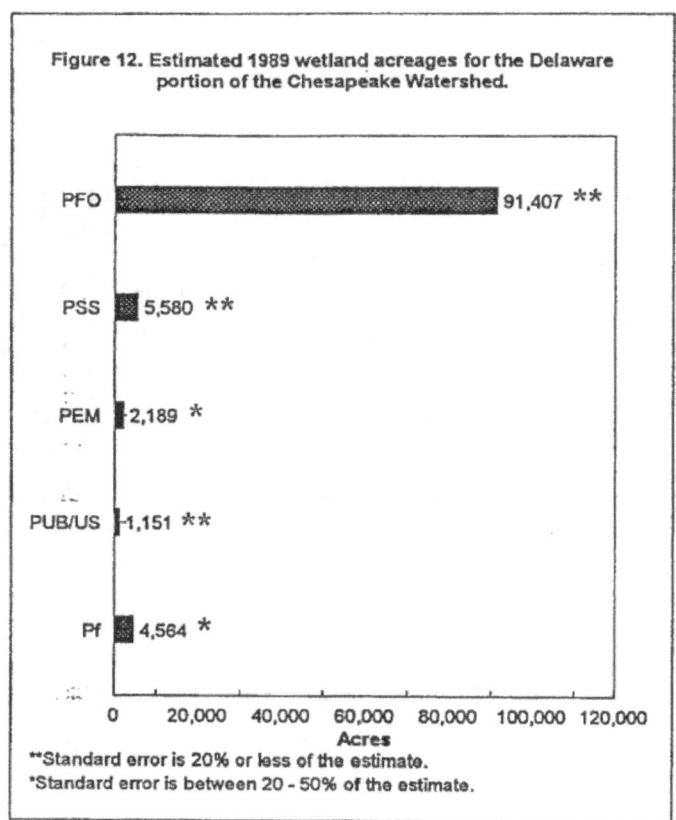

Figure 12. Estimated 1989 wetland acreages for the Delaware portion of the Chesapeake Watershed.

**Standard error is 20% or less of the estimate.
*Standard error is between 20 - 50% of the estimate.

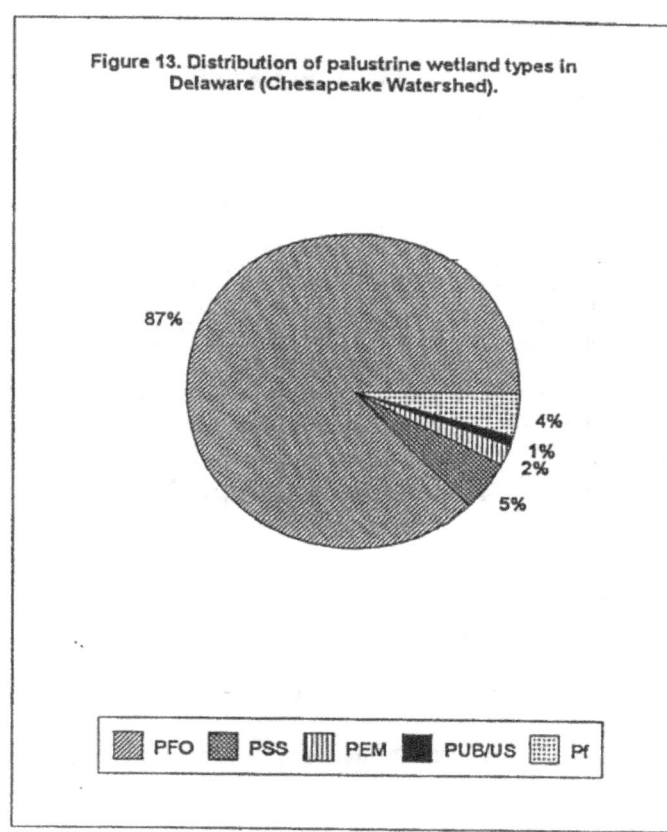

Figure 13. Distribution of palustrine wetland types in Delaware (Chesapeake Watershed).

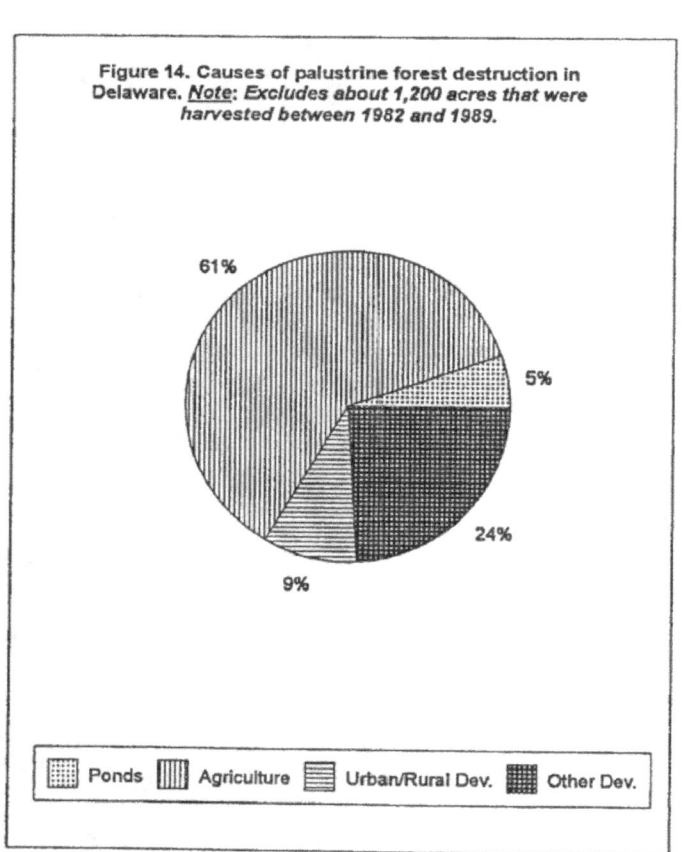

Figure 14. Causes of palustrine forest destruction in Delaware. *Note: Excludes about 1,200 acres that were harvested between 1982 and 1989.*

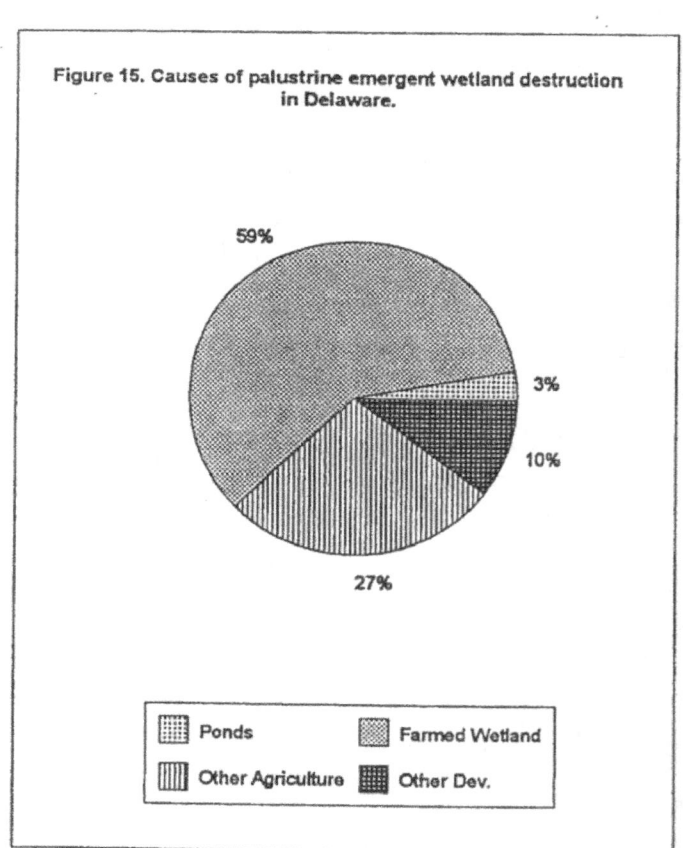

Figure 15. Causes of palustrine emergent wetland destruction in Delaware.

MARYLAND

Study findings for the Maryland portion of the Chesapeake Watershed are presented in Table 15, Figures 16-21, and in the following discussion. This 8,744-square mile area represents about 14 percent of the Watershed, excluding 2,275-square miles of estuarine wetlands and waters. It also represents about 90 percent of the state of Maryland.

Current Status

This portion of Maryland had about 440,000 acres of wetlands in 1989 (Figure 16). This acreage represents an area slightly larger than Frederick County. Palustrine wetlands cover roughly 324,000 acres, representing about 6 percent of the subject area's land mass. Palustrine forests, with 262,127 acres (7.2% SE), account for about 80 percent of the freshwater wetlands in this region (Figure 17). About 8 percent of Maryland's palustrine forests are significantly impacted by ditching and channelization (22,183 acres, 19.7% SE) (Table 9). Estuarine wetlands total about 120,000 acres. Eighty percent of these wetlands are emergent wetlands (Figure 18). Wetland densities differ within the state by physiographic region, ranging from a high of 134.2 acres/square mile (or 21% of the land area) in the Potholes Region on the Eastern Shore to 5.0 acres/square mile in western Maryland (Appalachian Highlands) (see Table 8). Beaver influences were greatest in western Maryland where 68 percent of the state's beaver-modified wetlands were found (Table 10).

Recent Trends

From 1982 to 1989, Maryland experienced a net loss of 4,324 acres (16.3% SE) of palustrine vegetated wetlands and 562 acres (77.5% SE) of estuarine vegetated wetlands, and net gains of 1,074 acres (92.6% SE) of estuarine nonvegetated wetlands (tidal flats) and 3,236 acres (25.6% SE) of palustrine nonvegetated wetlands (ponds). In addition, a net total of 2,062 acres (52.5% SE) of farmed wetlands were effectively drained and converted to upland agriculture. This represents about half of the farmed wetlands that existed in 1982. For vegetated wetlands, the figures represent a 1.4 percent loss of palustrine types and a 0.5 percent loss of estuarine types. Not all vegetated types, however, had net losses (Table 15); scrub-shrub wetlands showed net gains.

More acres of palustrine forests were destroyed than any other wetland type, with an estimated 2,534 acres (15.2% SE) converted to uplands or waterbodies between 1982 and 1989. Over 80 percent of these losses took place in the Lower Coastal Plain, mainly in the Pothole region (849 acres, 28.2% SE) and the rest of the Coastal Flats region (1,127 acres, 22.1% SE). An additional 437 acres (36.8% SE) of palustrine forests were destroyed on the Western Shore (Rolling Plain - Irregular Plains stratum). The main causes for palustrine forest destruction were agriculture (31%), pond construction (28%), and urban/rural development (22%) (Figure 19). Approximately 7,500 acres of palustrine forests were harvested for timber between 1982 and 1989. Logging impacts were greatest on the Eastern Shore (Table 13).

An estimated 2,370 acres (14.0% SE) of palustrine emergent wetlands were converted to uplands or waterbodies between 1982 and 1989. Nearly 72 percent of these losses occurred in the Lower Coastal Plain. Most of these losses took place in the Pothole region (911 acres destroyed, 22.1% SE) and in the rest of the Coastal Flats region (646 acres, 19.6% SE). An estimated 344 acres (39.8% SE) of these marshes and wet meadows were destroyed in the Piedmont region (Rolling Plain #1 stratum). Agricultural conversion of palustrine emergent wetlands was responsible for 63 percent of the losses of this type (Figure 20).

Despite a net gain overall, an estimated 454 acres (38.5% SE) of palustrine scrub-shrub wetlands were filled or permanently flooded. As with the emergent wetlands, most of the losses were in the Potholes region (257 acres, 63.0% SE) and the rest of the Coastal Flats region (159 acres, 39.0% SE).

Estuarine emergent wetlands were adversely affected by agricultural practices (including cropland associated with regulated shooting areas), coastal erosion and dredging, and urban and other development (Figure 21).

Table 15. Changes in specific types of vegetated wetlands in the Maryland portion of the Chesapeake Watershed (1982-1989).

Vegetated Wetland Type	1982 Acres	1989 Acres	Acres Changed to Other Veg Wetlands	Acres Gained From Veg Wetlands	Acres Destroyed	Acres Gained From Other Areas	Net Change
PFO	269,991 **	262,128 **	8,748 *	3,315 *	2,534 **	104	-7,863 *
PSS	15,674 **	20,852 **	3,568 *	9,102 *	454 *	98 *	+5,178 *
PEM	21,881 **	20,243 **	3,145 *	2,964 *	2,370 **	913 *	-1,638
E2EM	96,525 **	96,453 **	173 *	708	671 *	64	-72
E2SS	2,117 *	2,396 *	150	429 *	0	0	+279
E2FO	18,993 *	18,227 *	1,155	423	62	28	-766

**   Standard error is 20 percent or less than the estimate.

*   Standard error is less than 50 percent of the estimate, but greater than 20 percent of the estimate.

Note: Estimates without an asterisk have higher standard errors.

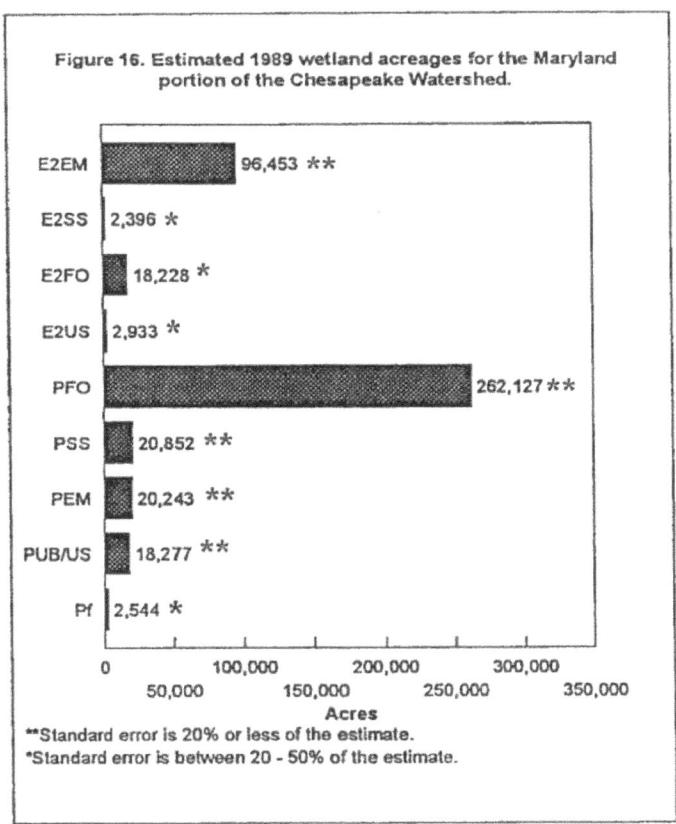

Figure 16. Estimated 1989 wetland acreages for the Maryland portion of the Chesapeake Watershed.

**Standard error is 20% or less of the estimate.
*Standard error is between 20 - 50% of the estimate.

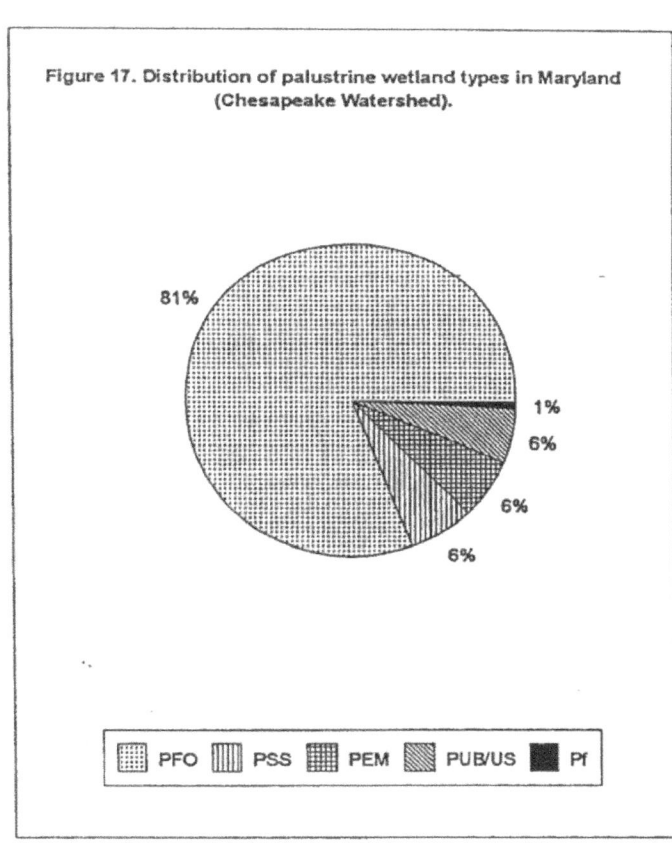

Figure 17. Distribution of palustrine wetland types in Maryland (Chesapeake Watershed).

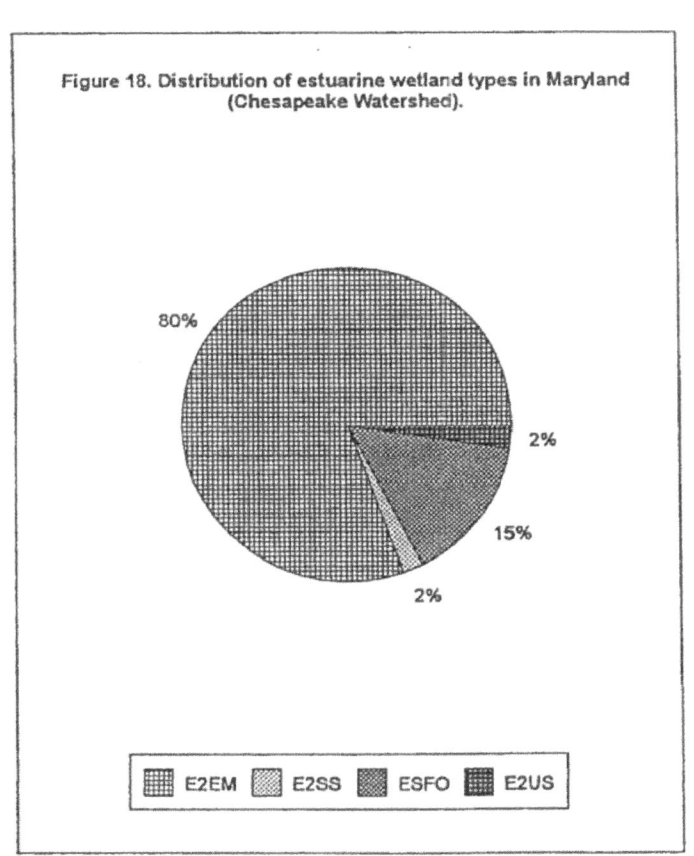

Figure 18. Distribution of estuarine wetland types in Maryland (Chesapeake Watershed).

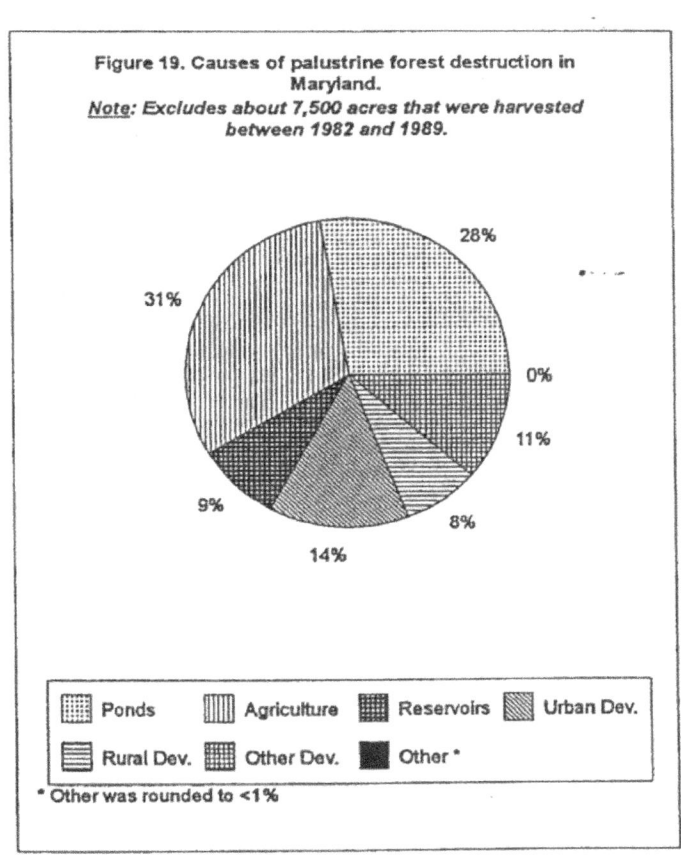

Figure 19. Causes of palustrine forest destruction in Maryland.
Note: Excludes about 7,500 acres that were harvested between 1982 and 1989.

* Other was rounded to <1%

41

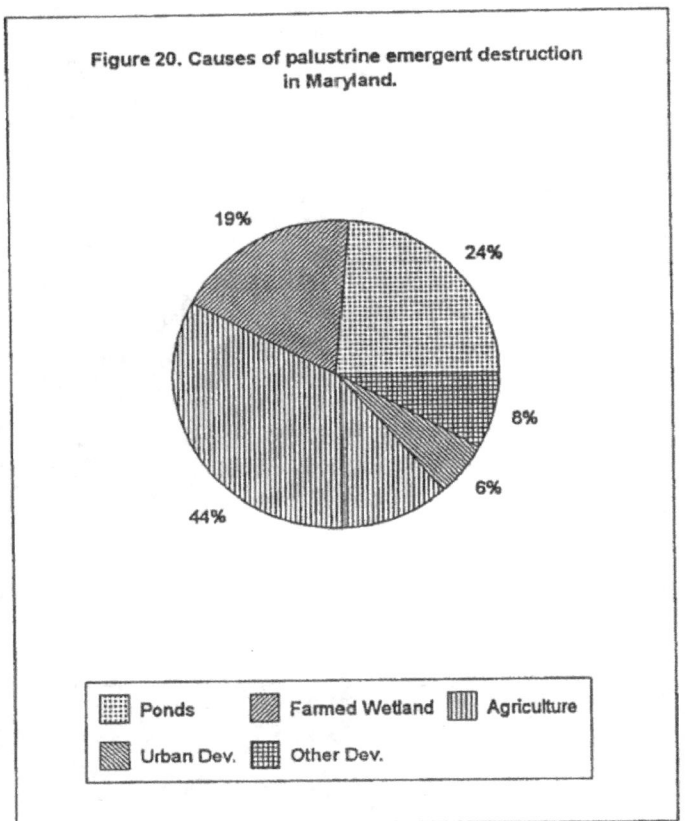

Figure 20. Causes of palustrine emergent destruction in Maryland.

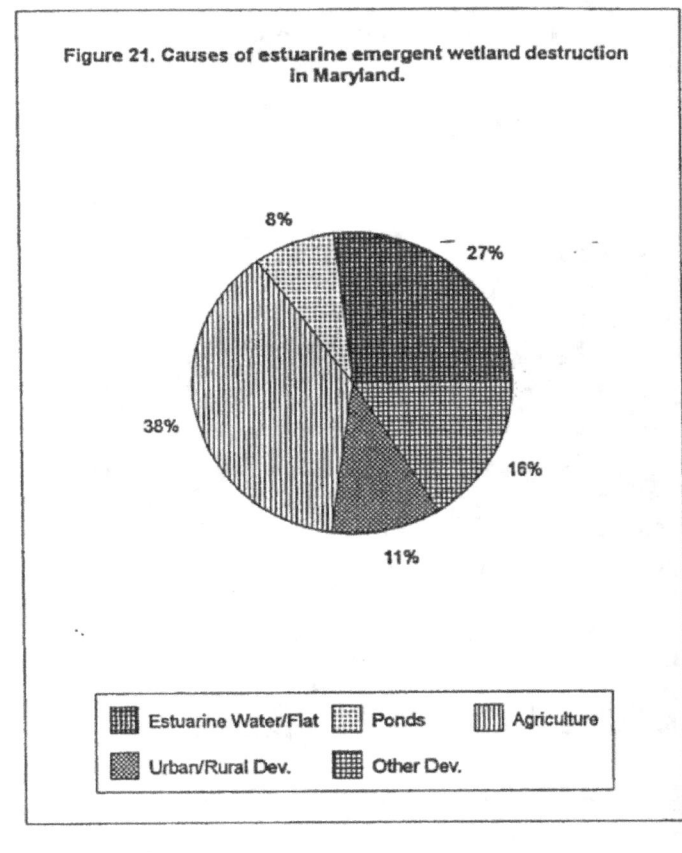

Figure 21. Causes of estuarine emergent wetland destruction in Maryland.

NEW YORK

Table 16 represents the study findings for the New York portion of the Watershed. This 6,181-square mile area occupies almost 10 percent of the Watershed. It also encompasses 14 percent of New York.

Current Status

Wetlands cover over 180,000 acres of this area which is about the size of Nassau County. This acreage represents about 5 percent of the surface area. Wetland density is 29.3 acres/square mile which is high for the Appalachian Highlands portion of the Chesapeake Watershed. This increased density is due to recent glaciation which created a landscape conducive to wetland formation. Palustrine forests are the predominant wetland type (77,737 acres, 75.1% SE) accounting for about 43 percent of the palustrine wetlands (Figures 22 and 23). Scrub-shrub wetlands and emergent wetlands are nearly equally abundant.

Recent Trends

There was no wetland alteration observed in the sample plots for this region. A modest gain in scrub-shrub wetlands came at the expense of emergent wetlands, presumably through natural succession. Pond acreage dropped slightly, with 99 acres (100% SE) becoming emergent wetlands.

Table 16. Changes in specific types of vegetated wetlands in the New York portion of the Chesapeake Watershed (1982-1989).

Vegetated Wetland Type	1982 Acres	1989 Acres	Acres Changed to Other Veg Wetlands	Acres Gained From Veg Wetlands	Acres Destroyed	Acres Gained From Other Areas	Net Change
PFO	77,737	77,737	0	0	0	0	0
PSS	44,704	45,594	0	890	0	0	+890
PEM	41,440 *	40,649 *	890	0	0	99	-791

**   Standard error is 20 percent or less than the estimate.

*   Standard error is less than 50 percent of the estimate, but greater than 20 percent of the estimate.

Note: Estimates without an asterisk have higher standard errors.

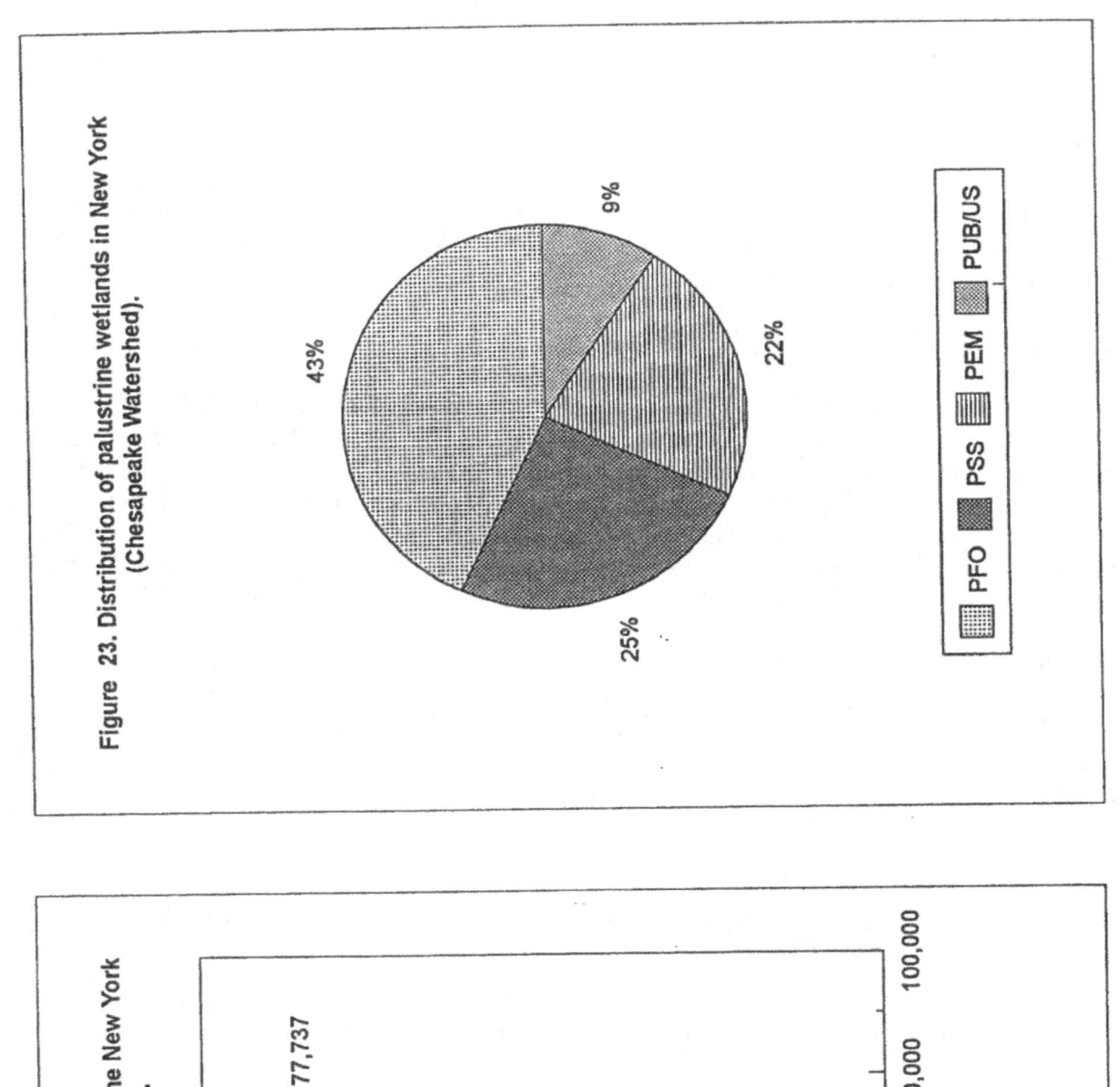

Figure 23. Distribution of palustrine wetlands in New York (Chesapeake Watershed).

43%

9%

22%

25%

PFO PSS PEM PUB/US

Figure 22. Estimated 1989 wetland acreages for the New York portion of the Chesapeake Watershed.

PFO — 77,737

PSS — 45,594

PEM — 40,649 *

PUB/US — 17,110

Acres

0   20,000   40,000   60,000   80,000   100,000

*Standard error is between 20 - 50% of the estimate. Other numbers have higher standard errors.

44

PENNSYLVANIA

Study findings for the Pennsylvania portion of the Watershed are presented in Table 17, Figures 24-27, and in the following discussion. This 22,478-square mile area represents about 36 percent of the Watershed's land surface area. It also occupies 50 percent of the Commonwealth of Pennsylvania.

Current Status

This area of the state had about 240,000 acres of wetlands in 1989, including more than 30,000 acres of ponds. These wetlands cover about 1.7 percent of the region's land surface area. Wetlands in the Pennsylvania portion of the Watershed represent an area about the size of Carbon County or Northampton County. Palustrine forests are the predominant type and account for half of the region's wetlands (Figures 24 and 25). Wetland densities vary across the state largely by physiographic region, ranging from high densities in glaciated northeastern Pennsylvania (16.9 to 40.3 acres/square mile or 2.6 to 6.3% of the land area) to 7.1 acres/square mile (or 1.1% of the area) in the Rolling Plain area of southeastern Pennsylvania (see Table 8). Pennsylvania had the second highest acreage of beaver-modified wetlands with almost 26,000 acres affected (Table 10).

Recent Trends

From 1982 to 1989, this area of Pennsylvania actually experienced a net increase of 4,683 acres (108.0% SE) in palustrine vegetated wetlands and a net loss of 3,411 acres (77.6% SE) of nonvegetated wetlands. The latter change was largely due to ponds succeeding into vegetated wetlands (1,398 acres, 22.7% SE, mainly emergent wetlands) and to filling ponds for unspecified development (760 acres, 37.0% SE). The net increase in palustrine vegetated wetlands was attributed to increases in forested and emergent wetlands. Nearly all of the gain in forested wetlands came from scrub-shrub wetlands, with 4,333 acres (23.5% SE) of the 1989 forested wetlands being the result of this type of succession. The gain in emergent wetlands was largely the result of marsh establishment in the shallow water zone of ponds and lakes (with estimated gains of 5,417 acres, 46.9% SE and 2,401 acres, 94.9% SE, respectively).

Despite these gains, existing emergent and scrub-shrub wetlands continued to be destroyed. An estimated 2,118 acres (27.5% SE) of emergent wetlands were converted to uplands and waterbodies. Over half of these losses took place in the Other Glaciated Northeast region where 1,270 acres (35.7% SE) were destroyed. The nonglaciated portion of the Appalachian Highlands region also lost considerable acreage: 596 acres (60.1% SE). An estimated 1,658 acres (52.0% SE) of scrub-shrub wetlands were destroyed, with 86 percent of the losses (1,421 acres, 60.5% SE) occurring in the nonglaciated region. Agriculture and pond construction accounted for 47 percent and 43 percent of the lost marshes and wet meadows (Figure 26). These factors were also the primary factors causing losses in scrub-shrub wetlands, with agriculture alone accounting for over 75 percent of the recent losses (1,260 acres, 67.7% SE) (Figure 27).

Table 17. Changes in specific types of vegetated wetlands in the Pennsylvania portion of the Chesapeake Watershed (1982-1989).

Vegetated Wetland Type	1982 Acres	1989 Acres	Acres Changed to Other Veg Wetlands	Acres Gained From Veg Wetlands	Acres Destroyed	Acres Gained From Other Areas	Net Change
PFO	117,552 **	120,100 **	1,693	4,341 *	200 *	100	+2,548
PSS	46,970 *	46,050 *	6,021 *	6,581 *	1,658	178	-920
PEM	39,404 **	42,459 *	5,652 *	2,444 *	2,118 *	8,381	+3,055

**   Standard error is 20 percent or less than the estimate.

*   Standard error is less than 50 percent of the estimate, but greater than 20 percent of the estimate.

Note: Estimates without an asterisk have higher standard errors.

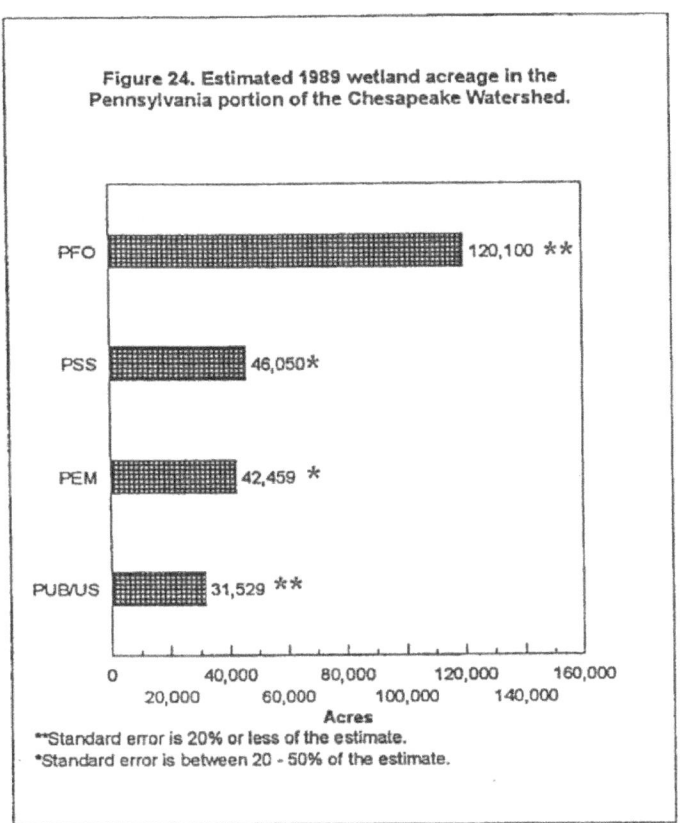

Figure 24. Estimated 1989 wetland acreage in the Pennsylvania portion of the Chesapeake Watershed.

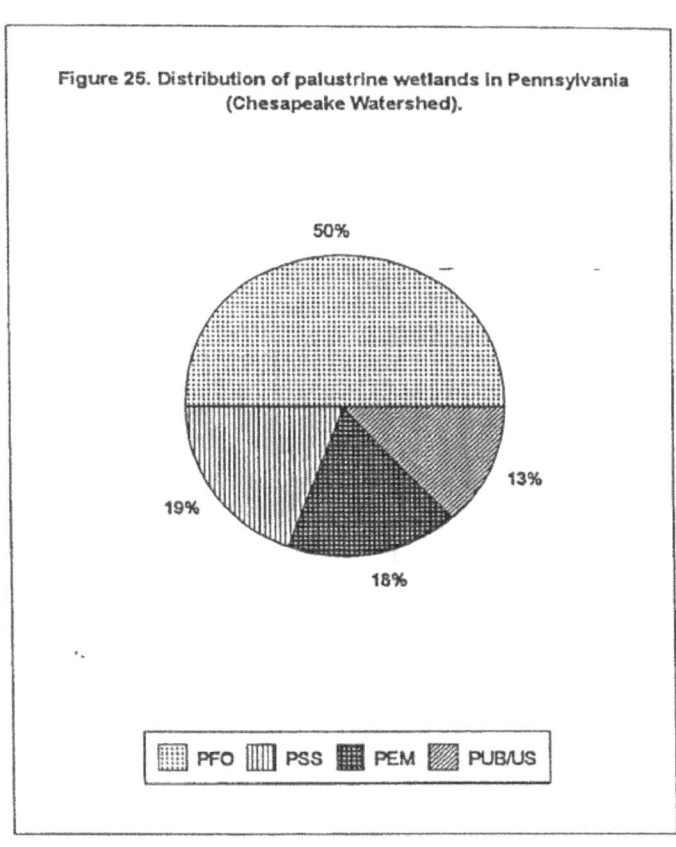

Figure 25. Distribution of palustrine wetlands in Pennsylvania (Chesapeake Watershed).

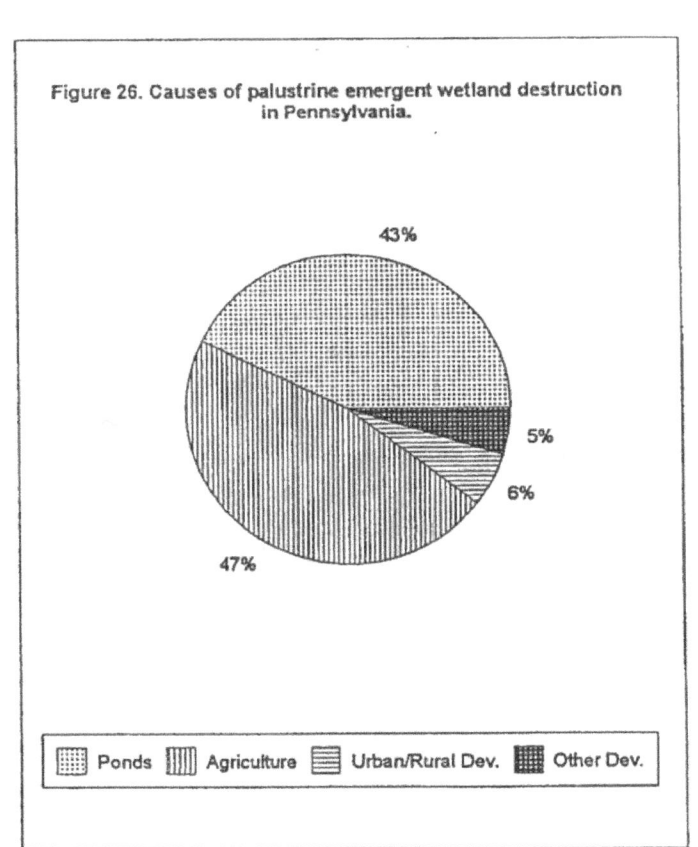

Figure 26. Causes of palustrine emergent wetland destruction in Pennsylvania.

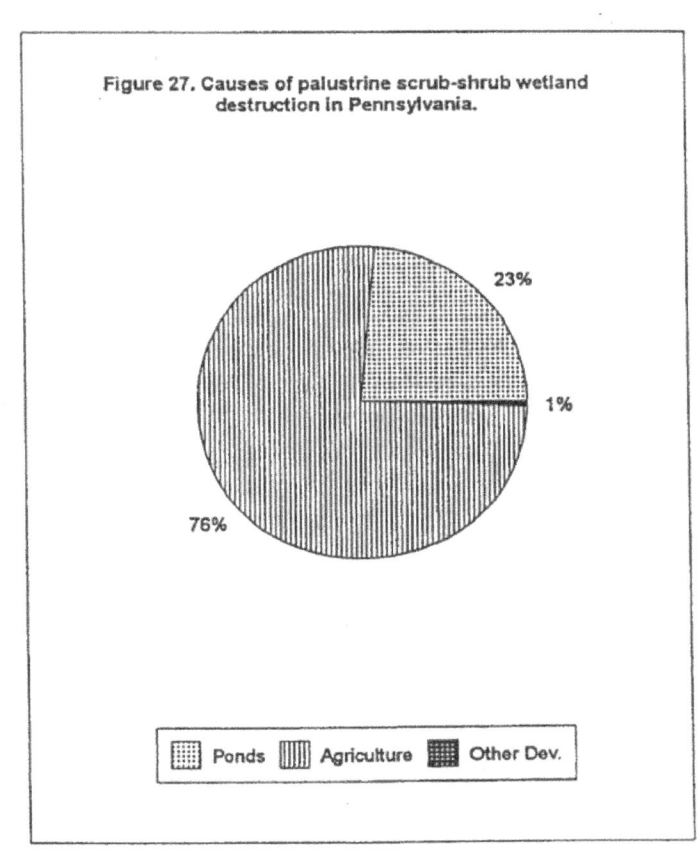

Figure 27. Causes of palustrine scrub-shrub wetland destruction in Pennsylvania.

47

VIRGINIA

Table 18, Figures 28-34, and the following discussion summarize study findings for the Virginia portion of the Watershed. This 21,359-square mile area represents about 34 percent of the Watershed, including 1,536-square miles of estuarine wetlands and waters. It also encompasses about 54 percent of Virginia.

Current Status

This area of Virginia had roughly 670,000 acres of wetlands in 1989. Wetland acreage amounts to an area about the size of Chesapeake, Norfolk, Virginia Beach, and Suffolk combined, or the size of Loudoun County. Palustrine wetlands cover about 586,000 acres. Palustrine forests, with 430,013 acres (9.8% SE) are the predominant type accounting for nearly two-thirds of the area's wetlands and for about 73 percent of the area's freshwater wetlands (Figures 28 and 29). This area of Virginia had more than 27,500 acres of ditched wetlands, mostly palustrine forests (19,702 acres, 45.0% SE). Most of the ditching and channelization occurred in eastern Virginia (Table 9). Virginia had the greatest extent of beaver-modified wetlands in the Watershed, with almost 68,000 acres affected (Table 10). Most of the beaver activity was in the Rolling Plain. Estuarine wetlands total approximately 85,000 acres, with the emergent type being most abundant (73,362 acres, 18.3% SE or 87% of the estuarine wetlands) (Figure 30). Wetland densities differ throughout the state by physiographic region ranging from a high of 112.2 wetland acres/square mile (or 17.5% of the land area) in the Coastal Flats area outside of the Southeast Metro region (Norfolk-Hampton) to a low of 3.0 acres/square mile (or 0.5% of the land area) in the western mountains (Appalachian Highlands) (see Table 8).

Recent Trends

From 1982 to 1989, Virginia had net losses in all vegetated wetland types and a net gain in pond acreage (4,938 acres, 23.6% SE). Palustrine vegetated wetlands declined by 17,472 acres (65.1% SE), while estuarine vegetated wetlands dropped by only 344 acres (57.3% SE).

An estimated 10,857 acres (56.0% SE) of forested wetlands were destroyed. Almost two-thirds (7,024 acres, 85.9% SE) of these losses took place in the Piedmont region (Rolling Plains #1 stratum), and nearly 20 percent (2,609 acres, 32.2% SE) of the total palustrine forest loss occurred in the Southeast Metro region (Norfolk-Hampton area). Also significant was the loss of 1,270 acres (28.3% SE) of forested wetlands in the Upper Coastal Plain (Rolling Plain #2 stratum). The main causes for palustrine forest destruction were reservoir construction (60%), urban and rural development (17%), and pond construction (17%) (Figure 31). Over 9,000 acres of palustrine forests were harvested for timber during the study interval. These wetlands became other vegetated types with the removal of the tree canopy. Logging impacts were heaviest in eastern Virginia (see Table 13). Ditching and channelization of palustrine forested wetlands increased by 4,668 acres (74.4% SE) during the study interval. This activity was concentrated in eastern Virginia, outside of the Norfolk-Hampton area.

Of the estimated 8,427 acres (81.2% SE) of scrub-shrub wetlands destroyed, almost 90 percent were located in the Piedmont region (Rolling Plain #1). Reservoir construction also took a heavy toll on scrub-shrub wetlands, accounting for about 82 percent of the recent losses, while pond construction accounted for much of the remaining losses (13%) (Figure 32).

An estimated 4,190 acres (31.7% SE) of palustrine emergent wetlands were converted to drylands and waterbodies. Slightly more than half of these losses occurred in the Piedmont region where 1,462 acres (47.9% SE) were destroyed. Many of these wetlands were also lost in the Appalachian Highlands region of western Virginia where 1,462 acres (56.1% SE) were converted. Palustrine emergent wetlands were mostly converted to cropland (35%), ponds (32%), and reservoirs (23%) (Figure 33).

Of the estuarine wetlands, salt and brackish marshes experienced the greatest recent losses, with 412 acres (40.0% SE) destroyed. These marshes were mainly converted to open water or tidal flats (presumably by a combination of factors including rising sea level, coastal subsidence, coastal erosion, and dredging) and to other development (Figure 34).

Table 18. Changes in specific types of vegetated wetlands in the Virginia portion of the Chesapeake Watershed (1982-1989).

Vegetated Wetland Type	1982 Acres	1989 Acres	Acres Changed to Other Veg Wetlands	Acres Gained From Veg Wetlands	Acres Destroyed	Acres Gained From Other Areas	Net Change
PFO	436,596 **	430,013 **	12,948 **	14,008 *	10,857	3,214	-6,583
PSS	65,824 **	57,782 **	16,203 *	15,833 *	8,427	755 *	-8,042
PEM	56,072 **	53,226 **	8,581 *	7,957 **	4,190 *	1,968 *	-2,846
E2EM	73,784 **	73,362 **	106	32	412 *	64	-422 *
E2SS	1,114 *	1,298 *	45	160	0	69	+184
E2FO	4,792	4,686	151	45	0	0	-106

**   Standard error is 20 percent or less than the estimate.

*   Standard error is less than 50 percent of the estimate, but greater than 20 percent of the estimate.

Note: Estimates without an asterisk have higher standard errors.

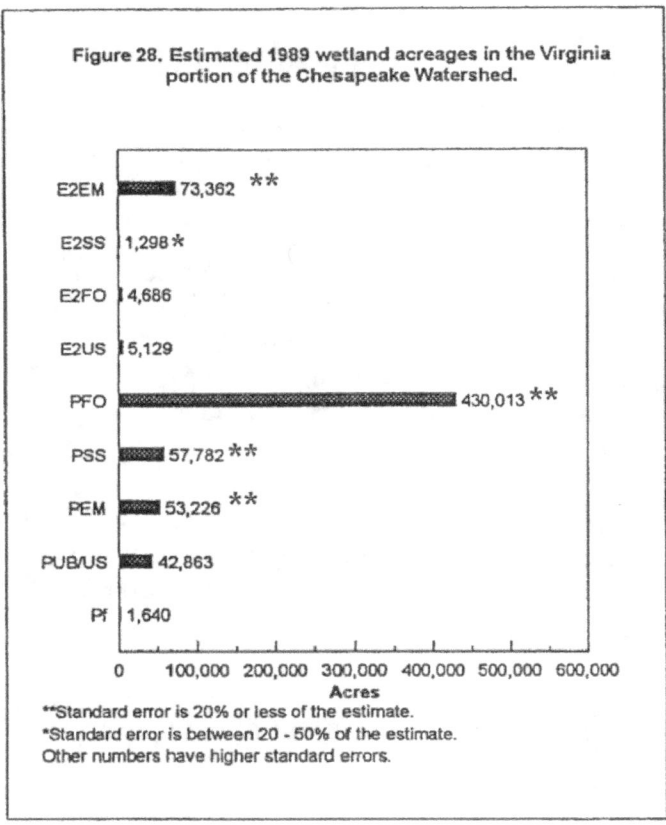

Figure 28. Estimated 1989 wetland acreages in the Virginia portion of the Chesapeake Watershed.

**Standard error is 20% or less of the estimate.
*Standard error is between 20 - 50% of the estimate.
Other numbers have higher standard errors.

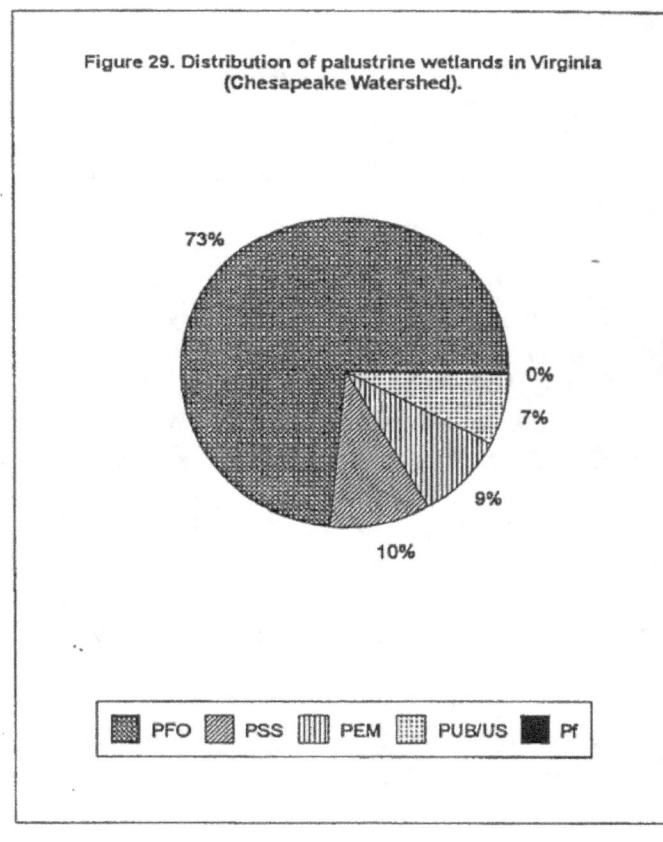

Figure 29. Distribution of palustrine wetlands in Virginia (Chesapeake Watershed).

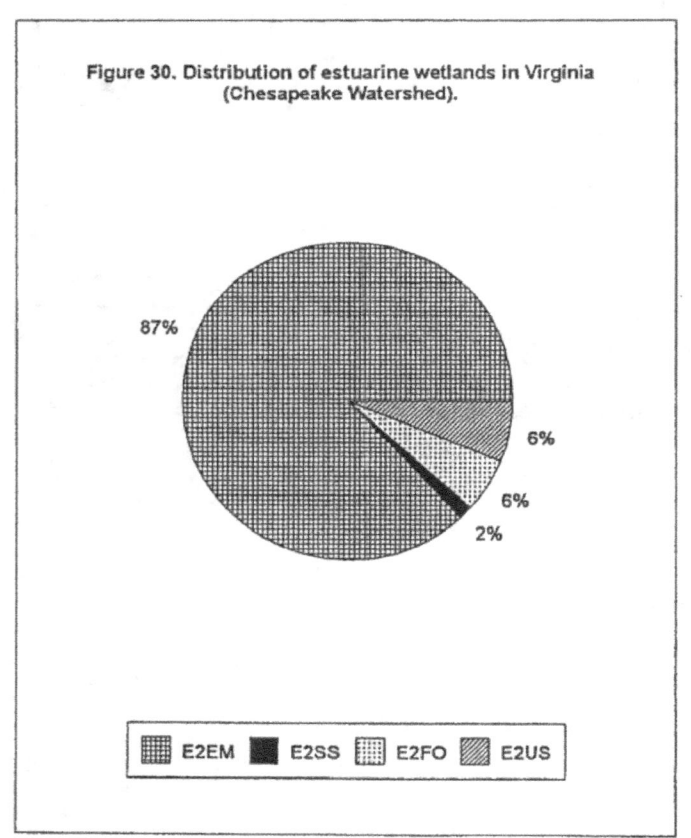

Figure 30. Distribution of estuarine wetlands in Virginia (Chesapeake Watershed).

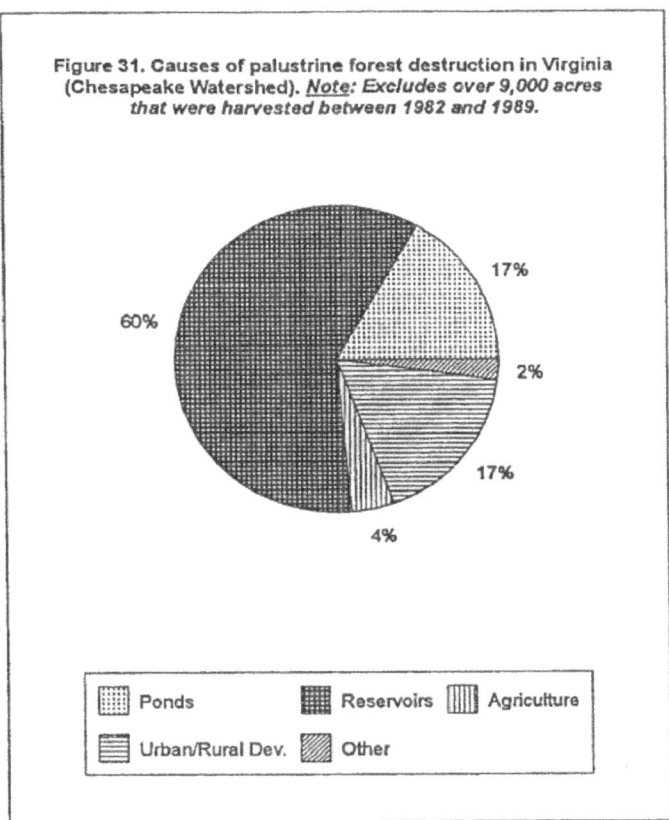

Figure 31. Causes of palustrine forest destruction in Virginia (Chesapeake Watershed). *Note: Excludes over 9,000 acres that were harvested between 1982 and 1989.*

60%
17%
2%
17%
4%

Ponds   Reservoirs   Agriculture
Urban/Rural Dev.   Other

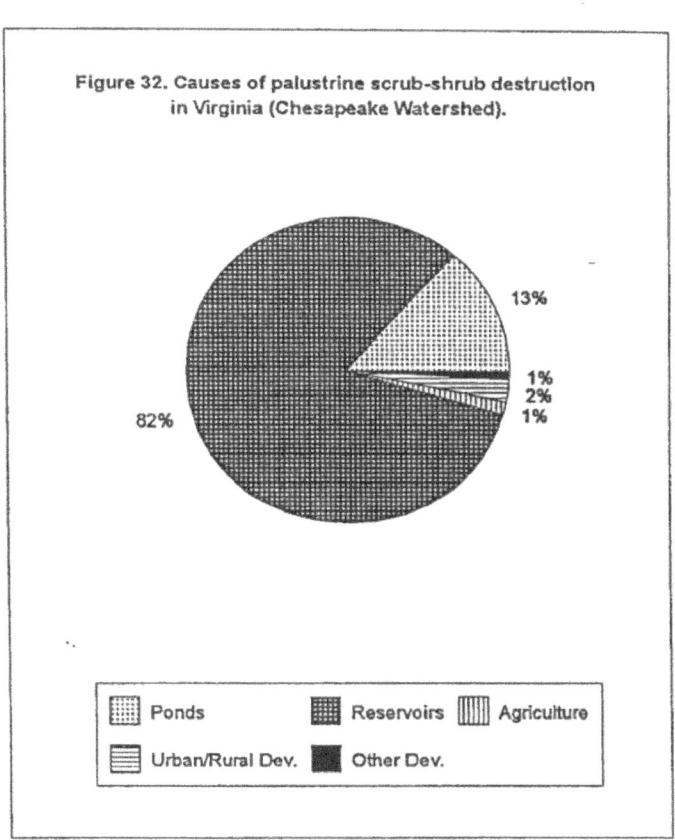

Figure 32. Causes of palustrine scrub-shrub destruction in Virginia (Chesapeake Watershed).

13%
1%
2%
1%
82%

Ponds   Reservoirs   Agriculture
Urban/Rural Dev.   Other Dev.

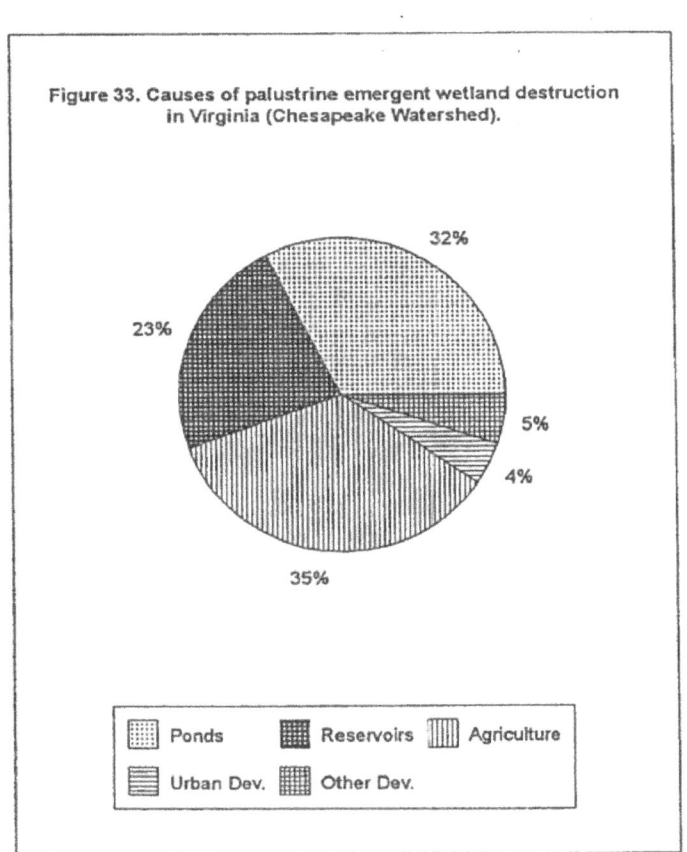

Figure 33. Causes of palustrine emergent wetland destruction in Virginia (Chesapeake Watershed).

32%
23%
5%
4%
35%

Ponds   Reservoirs   Agriculture
Urban Dev.   Other Dev.

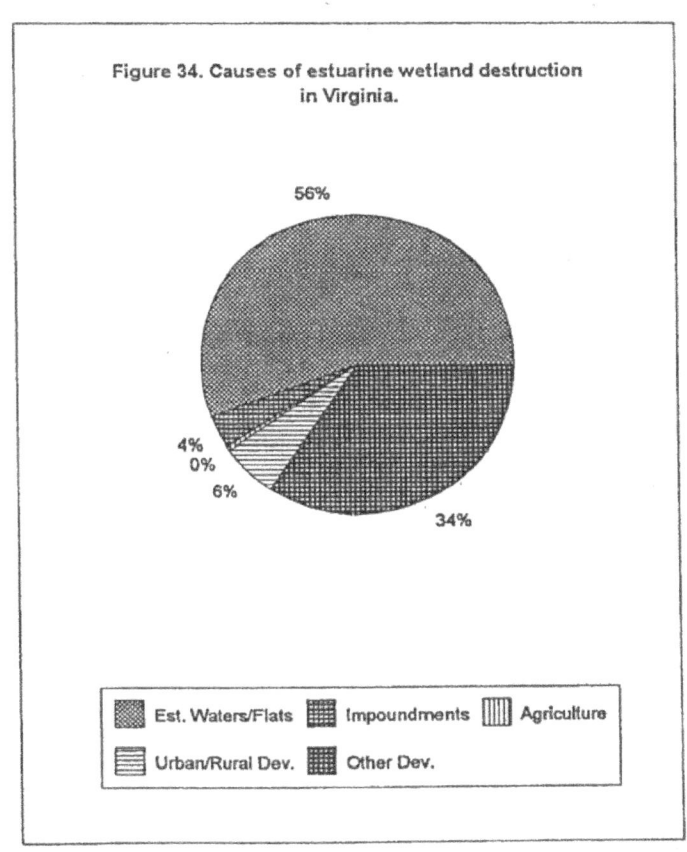

Figure 34. Causes of estuarine wetland destruction in Virginia.

56%
4%
0%
6%
34%

Est. Waters/Flats   Impoundments   Agriculture
Urban/Rural Dev.   Other Dev.

WEST VIRGINIA

Study findings for the West Virginia portion of the Chesapeake Watershed are given in Table 19, Figures 35 and 36, and the following discussion. The 3,571-square mile area represents about 6 percent of the Watershed's land area. It also represents about 15 percent of West Virginia.

Current Status

Almost 22,000 acres of wetlands were present here in 1989, including roughly 4,000 acres of ponds. Wetlands occupy about 1 percent of the land area. The wetlands are dominated by palustrine emergent and forested wetlands with 8,450 acres (67.8% SE) and 7,954 acres (38.4% SE), respectively (Figures 35 and 36). The average density of wetlands in the area was 6.2 acres/square mile.

Recent Trends

Between 1982 and 1989, there were net gains in palustrine forested and scrub-shrub wetlands and in ponds, but net losses of emergent wetlands. Palustrine forested wetlands increased by 288 acres (68.8% SE) mainly from scrub-shrub wetlands and other land. Scrub-shrub wetlands also showed a net gain of 288 acres (113.5% SE) due mainly from emergent wetlands which dropped by 288 acres (63.9% SE). No agricultural conversion or urban-rural development was detected.

Table 19. Changes in specific types of vegetated wetlands in the West Virginia portion of the Chesapeake Watershed (1982-1989).

Vegetated Wetland Type	1982 Acres	1989 Acres	Acres Changed to Other Veg Wetlands	Acres Gained From Veg Wetlands	Acres Destroyed	Acres Gained From Other Areas	Net Change
PFO	7,666 *	7,954 *	0	112	0	176	+288
PSS	1,312	1,600	112	336	0	64	+288
PEM	8,738	8,450	336	0	16	64	-288

**   Standard error is 20 percent or less than the estimate.

*   Standard error is less than 50 percent of the estimate, but greater than 20 percent of the estimate.

Note: Estimates without an asterisk have higher standard errors.

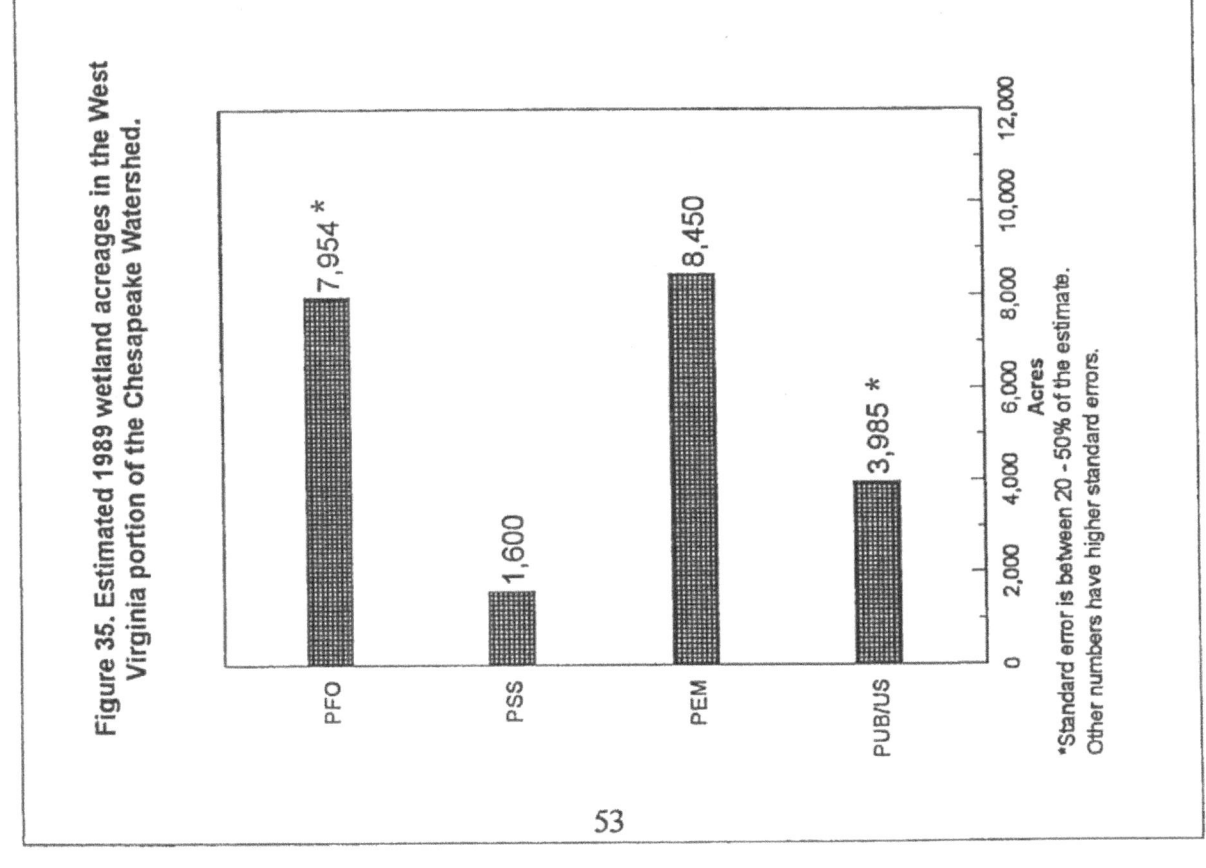

Figure 36. Distribution of palustrine wetlands in West Virginia (Chesapeake Watershed).

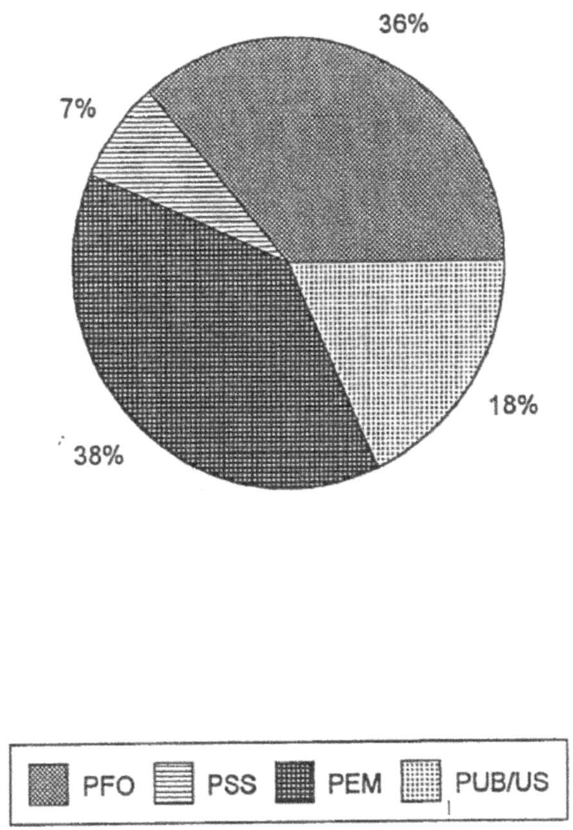

36%

18%

7%

38%

PFO   PSS   PEM   PUB/US

Figure 35. Estimated 1989 wetland acreages in the West Virginia portion of the Chesapeake Watershed.

PFO   7,954 *

PSS   1,600

PEM   8,450

PUB/US   3,985 *

0   2,000   4,000   6,000   8,000   10,000   12,000
Acres

*Standard error is between 20 - 50% of the estimate.
Other numbers have higher standard errors.

WETLAND LOSS HOTSPOTS

This study has identified several areas that experienced enormous human-induced losses of vegetated wetlands between 1982 and 1989. These areas called "wetland loss hotspots" are in need of increased wetland protection to minimize future losses. Listed below are the hotspots for the Chesapeake Watershed. Note that the areas are not listed in order of importance, since wetlands in all these areas need better protection over that received prior to 1989.

1.   **Southeastern Virginia.** This hotspot represents the greater Hampton-Norfolk-Virginia Beach area where there has been tremendous growth in the past two decades. Over 2,000 acres of palustrine forests were converted to dryland and waterbodies. This represents about a 5 percent loss of the 1982 forested wetlands in this locale. This estimated loss is actually conservative since a detailed assessment of wetland changes during the same time period for 12 quads in this area showed that nearly 4,000 acres of palustrine forests were converted to upland mainly for housing developments and agriculture (see Appendix B for summary findings; Tiner and Foulis 1994). The forested wetlands most affected were seasonally saturated and temporarily flooded types. Many of these wetlands are still not being regulated by the Federal government, since they fail to meet all the requirements for wetland as defined by the Corps of Engineers Wetlands Delineation Manual (Environmental Laboratory 1987). Although wet through winter, they do not appear to be wet for a sufficient period during the "growing season" used in the manual.

2.   **Piedmont region of Virginia.** This area extends west of Richmond to the Blue Ridge Mountains (see Figure 2). During the study period, an estimated almost 17,000 acres of palustrine vegetated wetlands were destroyed: 2,159 acres (47.9% SE) of emergent wetlands, 7,462 acres (91.7% SE) of scrub-shrub wetlands, and 7,024 acres (85.9% SE) of forested wetlands. These losses represent 10 percent of the emergent wetlands, 23 percent of the scrub-shrub wetlands, and 4 percent of the forested wetlands that existed in 1982. Reservoir/lake construction in this area was responsible for over 80 percent of these estimated losses, while pond construction accounted for 10 percent of the total losses.

3.   **Eastern Shore of Maryland.** Over 4,000 acres of palustrine vegetated wetlands were converted to dryland and waterbodies during the 7-year study period. Half of the losses involved forested wetlands, while 40 percent were losses of emergent wetlands. The latter losses of about 1,700 acres represent a 17 percent loss of the 1982 emergent wetlands. Most of these losses were attributed to agriculture and pond construction. The palustrine forest losses were the result of numerous human activities including agriculture, pond/reservoir/lake construction, urban/rural development, and other human actions. It was undetermined whether the agricultural conversions of wetlands occurred prior to or after implementation of the Swampbuster provision of the Food Security Act of 1985. The appropriate authorities may want to investigate potential

violations. Forested wetlands in this area were also subjected to significant timber harvest with over 7,000 acres affected between 1982 and 1989.

4. **Western Delaware.** This area represents about 37 percent of the state (see Figure 2). Between 1982 and 1989, nearly 2,000 acres of palustrine emergent wetlands were destroyed, representing almost half of the marshes and wet meadows that were present in 1982. Most of these losses were due to agricultural conversion. Almost 680 acres of palustrine forests were converted to drylands and waterbodies, with most converted to farmland. As with hotspot #3, it is uncertain whether these agricultural conversions of wetlands occurred before or after the Swampbuster starting date of December 23, 1985. Again, responsible agencies may want to investigate potential violations.

5. **Upper Coastal Plain of Virginia.** This area lies approximately east of Richmond (part of the Rolling Plain stratum, see Figure 2). During the 7-year study period, almost 2,000 acres (1,931 acres, 21.0% SE) of palustrine vegetated methods were converted to drylands and waterbodies. Most of the losses involved palustrine forests (1,270 acres, 28.3% SE). Over half of these forested wetland losses were due to pond construction.

6. **Western Virginia - the Blue Ridge and Appalachians.** This area experienced a 34 percent loss of its 1982 base of emergent wetlands. Nearly 1,500 acres (1,462 acres, 56.1% SE) of the marshes and wet meadows were destroyed. Nearly 80 percent of this loss was caused by agricultural conversion.

7. **Northeastern Pennsylvania.** This area falls mostly within Susquehanna, Bradford, and Tioga Counties, and for the study was called the Other Glaciated Northeast (see Figure 2). An estimated 1,270 acres (35.7% SE) of palustrine emergent wetlands were converted to drylands and waterbodies during the study period. This represents a 10 percent loss of the marshes and wet meadows that existed in 1982. Slightly more than half of the losses was due to pond construction while agricultural conversion was responsible for 40 percent of the losses.

DISCUSSION

An earlier study by Tiner and Finn (1986) was designed to evaluate wetland changes within the five-state area that represents the geographic limits of EPA Region III. The Chesapeake Watershed largely falls within this area, but also extends into New York State. The findings from this study for the Chesapeake Watershed were derived from wetland trends data from sample plots within the Watershed, excluding New York where no data were collected. The current study utilized these plots, but additional plots were selected with an attempt to improve the reliability of the estimates (i.e., lower the standard error) and to include some plots within the New York portion of the Watershed. Improved resolution of the late 1980s/early 1990s photography led to detection of pre-existing wetlands that had not been interpreted on the earlier photography. Changes in study design and improved wetland photointerpretation undoubtedly had a significant impact on the acreage estimates reported for 1982 when compared to the earlier trend study (Tiner and Finn 1986). The earlier study tended to underestimate the extent of palustrine forested wetlands. Therefore, comparison of the estimated totals for each wetland type is not appropriate, especially for palustrine forested wetlands. The latter were conservatively mapped in the earlier study due to the use of black and white photography for the 1950s and 1:58,000 color infrared photography for 1980. The use of 1:40,000 color infrared photography and the temporal difference in the wetness reflected on this imagery facilitated the identification of forested wetlands. With this in mind, let us compare the recent trends with the 1950s to late 70s/early 80s trends reported by Tiner and Finn (1986).

Comparing the results of the present study with an earlier study reveals some interesting changes in the magnitude of wetland conversion and in the factors responsible for change in the Watershed. The Tiner and Finn study covered the period 1956 to 1979 for the Chesapeake Watershed for an interval of 23 years, while the present study represents a 7-year period. Thus, total acreage change in different wetlands is not comparable, but the findings can be reasonably contrasted when the change totals are expressed as average annual changes. Table 20 shows the changes in the average annual rates of change for the major wetland types based on the net gains or losses during the study period. Note that the earlier study did not include data for estuarine forested wetlands. This comparison identifies a decline in the annual loss rate for the following types: estuarine emergent wetlands, estuarine scrub-shrub wetlands (which most recently experienced a net annual gain), palustrine emergent wetlands (which had a tremendous decline in the loss rate), and palustrine scrub-shrub wetlands. Palustrine forested wetlands experienced an enormous (12-fold) rise in the net loss rate. Most of this change, however, was simply a change in wetland type due to timber harvesting practices (18,022 acres, 16.1% SE from 1982 to 1989; Table 13). This activity did not result in outright wetland destruction, since palustrine forests were converted to other vegetated wetland types. These gains had the effect of somewhat offsetting or minimizing the impact of activities that actually destroyed palustrine emergent and scrub-shrub wetlands. Timber harvest of forested wetlands appears to have accelerated during the 1980s. Pond acreage, while still on the rise, had a smaller annual gain than from the 50s to the 80s. The following subsections compare the 50s to 80s results with the more recent trends for major types of estuarine and palustrine wetlands.

Estuarine Wetlands

Losses of estuarine emergent and forested wetlands and gains in estuarine scrub-shrub and nonvegetated wetlands characterized the more recent time period, while losses in all vegetated types and a gain in nonvegetated types occurred from the 50s to the 80s (Table 20). Although salt and brackish marshes continued to be converted to other wetland types, deepwater habitats, or nonwetlands, average annual net losses were much less than the earlier loss rate: 71 acres versus 489 acres. The recent rate amounts to only 15 percent of the earlier rate, for an 85 percent decline in the average annual net loss rate of coastal marshes. Estuarine nonvegetated wetlands in contrast had an almost 3-fold increase in the average annual net gain rate from 47 acres to 135 acres. No data are available to compare trends in estuarine forested wetlands.

The status of estuarine wetlands appears to have dramatically improved during the past decade. Between 1956 and 1979, annual losses of estuarine vegetated wetlands averaged about 550 acres, with a net loss of 12,585 acres (41.5% SE). Most of the losses of estuarine emergent wetland involved conversion to estuarine water presumably by a combination of dredging, coastal erosion, rising sea level, and coastal subsidence (Figures 37 and 38). Urban and rural development of emergent wetlands was also much more significant prior to the adoption of state tidal wetland laws and strengthened Federal regulations under the Clean Water Act. Now estuarine wetlands are receiving better protection than any other wetland type in the Chesapeake Watershed. The results of our study support this. By comparing the effect of various destructive activities on estuarine emergent wetlands in Figures 37 and 38, one can easily see a dramatic shift in the significance of activities converting marsh to open water and filling marsh to urban and rural development. There was an 87 percent decline in the average annual loss due to activities converting marshes to open water and a 94 percent drop in filling marshes for urban and rural development. The development that did occur appears to be, at least in part, in areas beyond state jurisdiction. For Maryland, field inspections of selected sites on Kent Island determined that the filled marshes were former open marsh disposal areas dominated by common reed (Phragmites australis) that were not contained within the boundaries of tidal wetlands on the state's official regulatory maps. Overall for the study period, destruction of estuarine emergent wetlands dropped by 82 percent. Given that dredging and filling activities of estuarine wetlands are strictly controlled by state and Federal regulatory agencies, the tremendous decline in losses to open water and to development can, with high likelihood, be attributed to the success of these programs.

Palustrine Wetlands

The general trend for palustrine wetlands was a continuation of the earlier trend with net losses of all vegetated types and a net gain in nonvegetated wetlands (ponds) characterizing both periods. However, there were significant differences in the average annual changes (Table 20 and Figures 39 through 44) and the factors responsible for them.

Despite the existence of Federal wetland regulatory programs for implementing the Clean Water Act, nontidal freshwater wetlands continued to experience enormous losses. The magnitude of these changes points to a potentially serious resource management issue.

Figures 39 through 44 compare the causes and acreage effects for losses (conversion to nonwetlands and waterbodies) of palustrine forested, scrub-shrub, and emergent wetlands in the Chesapeake Watershed.

Actual losses of palustrine forests increased by about 30 percent with almost a 30-fold increase in losses due to reservoir/lake construction, a 3-fold increase in losses from urban and rural development, and a 17-fold increase in losses due to pond construction (Figures 39 and 40). Conversion of palustrine forests to cropland remained more or less the same.

Scrub-shrub wetlands experienced an almost 150 percent increase in losses to drylands and waterbodies, mainly due to reservoir/lake construction whose adverse impact increased 10-fold (Figures 41 and 42). Impacts from development activities declined markedly for these wetlands, but agricultural impacts rose dramatically (i.e., a 3-fold increase in the loss rate). Conversion of scrub-shrub wetlands to ponds remained similar to the rate prior to strengthened Federal regulations.

The status of palustrine emergent wetlands did not appear to worsen as much as for the other palustrine vegetated types. While the urban and rural development impacts declined by over 70 percent, agricultural conversion increased by more than 200 acres per year which represents a 37 percent increase in its adverse effects on wetlands (Figures 43 and 44). Reservoir/lake construction also had a greater negative impact on emergent wetlands than it did from the 1950s to the 1980s.

Nearly two-thirds of the palustrine vegetated wetland losses occurred in Virginia where almost 23,500 acres were destroyed. Even when gains in wetlands were included, there was still a net loss of 17,635 acres (64.5% SE) of these wetlands in Virginia. The bulk of the remaining losses of palustrine vegetated wetlands took place in Maryland (about 5,400 acres or 15% of the Watershed's losses), Pennsylvania (almost 4,000 acres or 11%), and Delaware (about 3,200 acres or 9%). It was interesting to note, however, that during the more recent 7-year period, as much acreage was converted to urban land as during the entire 23-year period, about 2,500 acres versus about 2,400 acres, respectively. This suggests that palustrine forested wetlands are under increasing pressure for development. It appears that despite strengthened Federal wetland protection, significant forested wetland acreage (presumably seasonally saturated types) is falling outside of the Federal jurisdiction. Pennsylvania's wetland protection program includes these wetlands, but it is questionable whether Maryland's nontidal wetlands program now regulates activities in these seasonally saturated wetlands given that it recently changed its field procedures for identifying regulated wetlands by adopting the Corps manual. Virginia has no similar regulatory program, so all such wetlands are vulnerable, especially those in rapidly urbanizing areas, such as the Norfolk-Hampton area (see Appendix B for summary of how wetlands recently changed in this area).

Table 20. Comparison of wetland trends for certain types in the Chesapeake Watershed (1956 to 1979 versus 1982 to 1989). Early data from Tiner and Finn (1986). Numbers in parentheses are the standard error for the estimate (expressed as a percent of the estimate). Under the average annual net change rate category, gains are indicated by a "+" and losses by a "-". The data are based on the net changes which tend to understate the conversion of existing wetlands to dryland and deepwater habitats. Figures 37, 39, 41, and 43 better reflect these.

Wetland Type	Net Acreage Change 50s to 80s Trends	Average Annual Net Change	Net Acreage Change 80s to 90s Trends	Average Annual Net Change
Estuarine Emergent	-11,253 (46.7)	-489	-496 (*)	-71
Estuarine Scrub-Shrub	-1,330 (78.6)	-58	+463 (37.6)	+66
Estuarine Forested	No Data	NA	-871 (84.4)	-124
Estuarine Nonvegetated	+1,082 (87.8)	+47	+946 (*)	+135
Palustrine Emergent	-44,530 (19.8)	-1,936	-4,283 (*)	-612
Palustrine Scrub-Shrub	-5,986 (*)	-260	-961 (*)	-137
Palustrine Forested	-4,070 (*)	-177	-14,406 (41.5)	-2,058
Palustrine Nonvegetated (Ponds)	+57,044 (13.7)	+2,480	+5,634 (55.4)	+805

*Standard error equals or exceeds the estimated acreage.

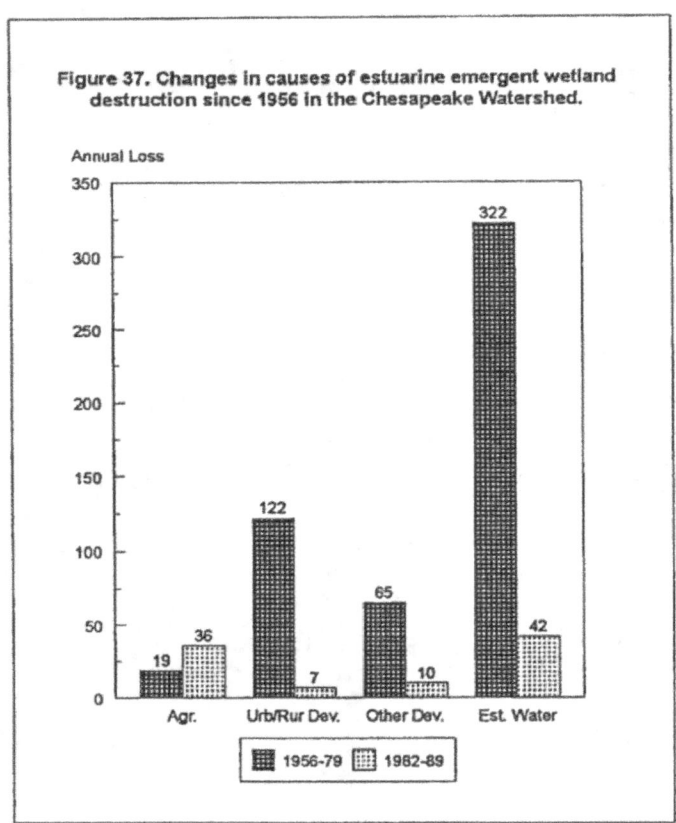

Figure 37. Changes in causes of estuarine emergent wetland destruction since 1956 in the Chesapeake Watershed.

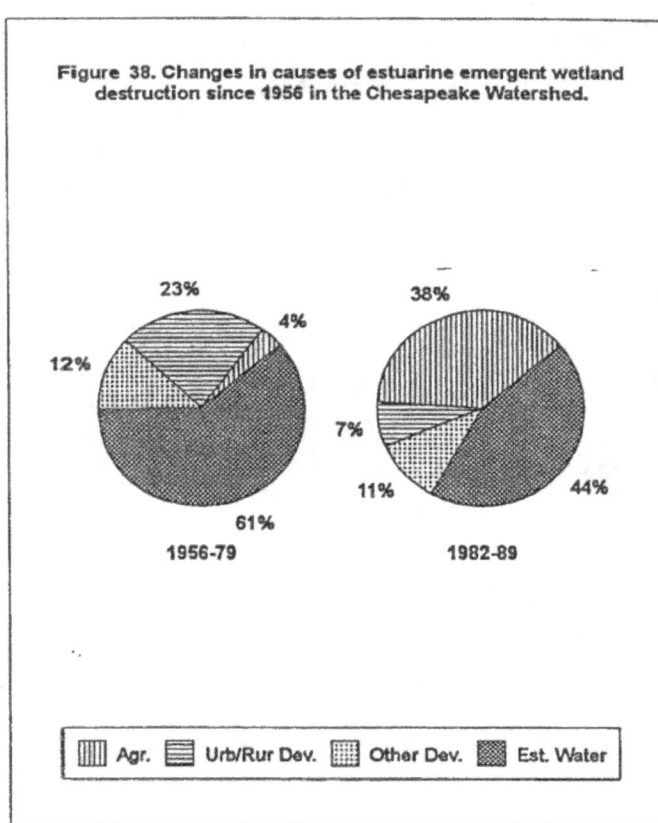

Figure 38. Changes in causes of estuarine emergent wetland destruction since 1956 in the Chesapeake Watershed.

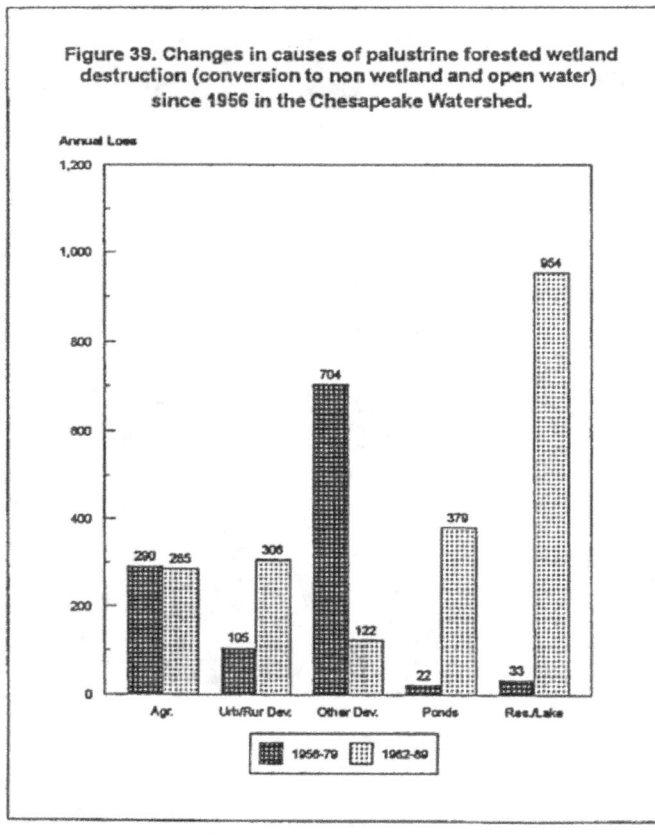

Figure 39. Changes in causes of palustrine forested wetland destruction (conversion to non wetland and open water) since 1956 in the Chesapeake Watershed.

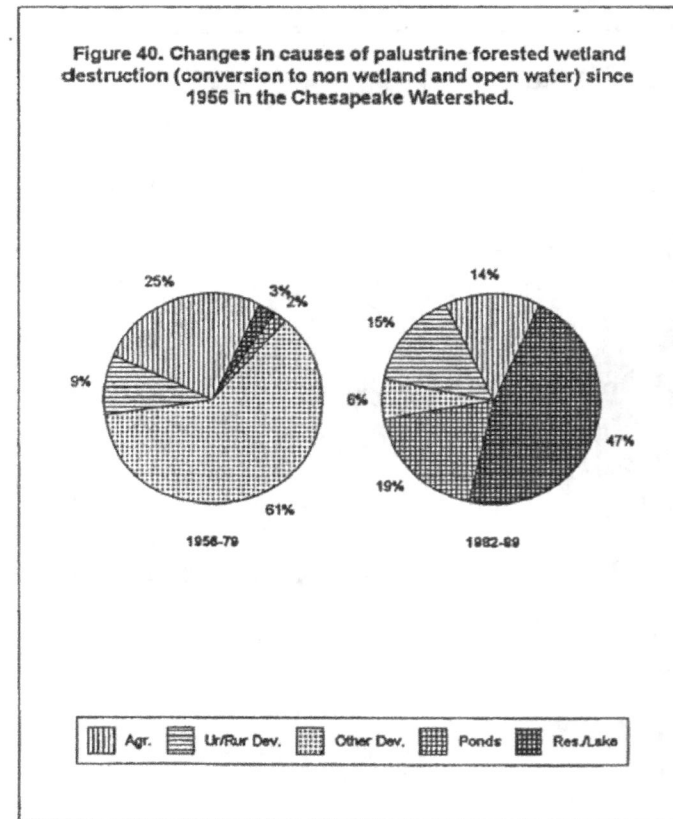

Figure 40. Changes in causes of palustrine forested wetland destruction (conversion to non wetland and open water) since 1956 in the Chesapeake Watershed.

Figure 41 . Changes in causes of palustrine scrub-shrub wetland destruction (conversion to non wetland and open water) since 1956 in the Chesapeake Watershed.

Annual Loss

Bar chart with values:
- Agr.: 80 (1956-79), 244 (1982-89)
- Urb/Rur Dev.: 119 (1956-79), 7 (1982-89)
- Other Dev.: 105 (1956-79), 27 (1982-89)
- Ponds: 210 (1956-79), 237 (1982-89)
- Res./Lake: 95 (1956-79), 986 (1982-89)

Legend: 1956-79, 1982-89

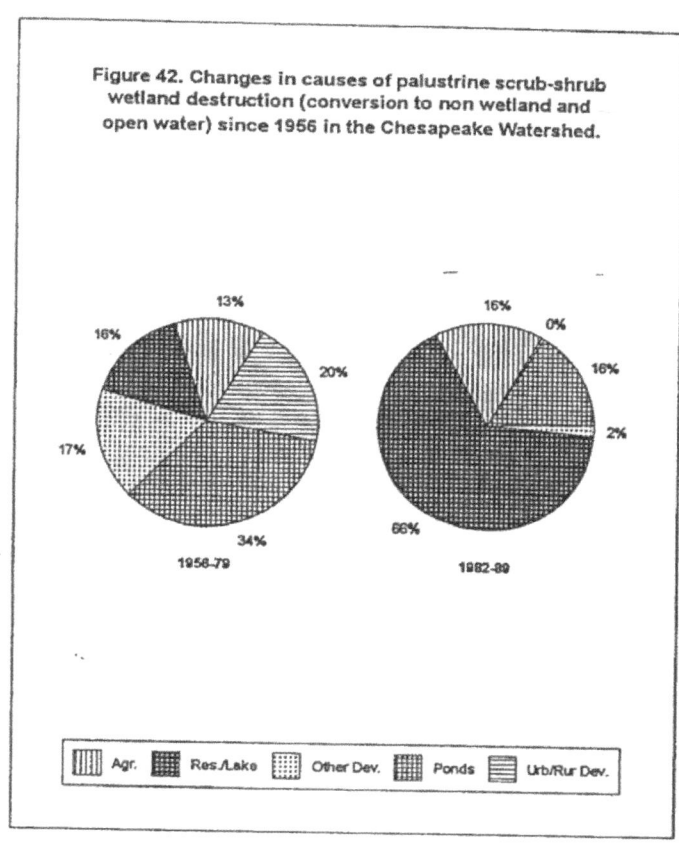

Figure 42. Changes in causes of palustrine scrub-shrub wetland destruction (conversion to non wetland and open water) since 1956 in the Chesapeake Watershed.

1956-79: 13%, 20%, 34%, 17%, 16%
1982-89: 16%, 0%, 16%, 2%, 66%

Legend: Agr., Res./Lake, Other Dev., Ponds, Urb/Rur Dev.

Figure 43. Changes in causes of palustrine emergent wetland destruction (conversion to non wetland and open water) since 1956 in the Chesapeake Watershed.

Annual Loss

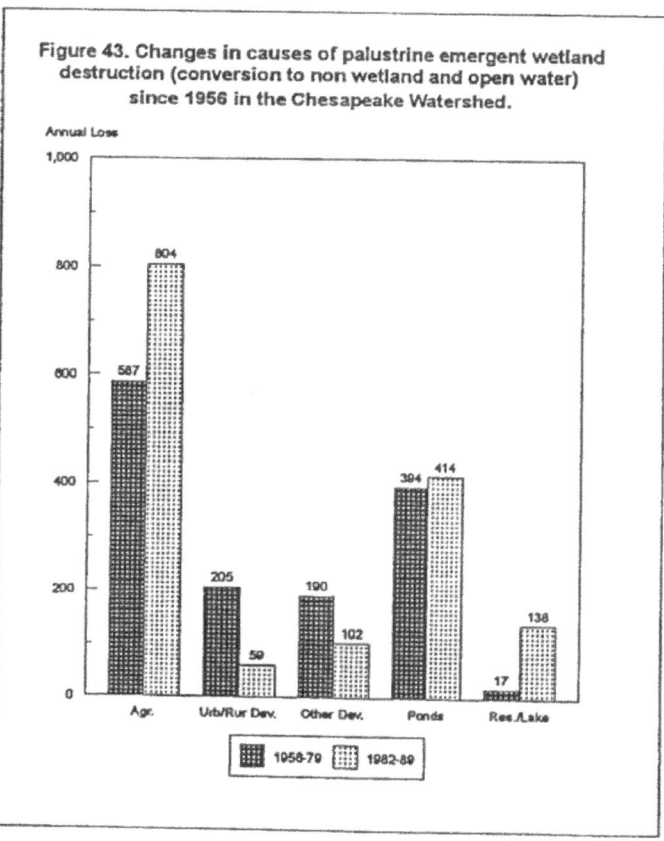

Bar chart with values:
- Agr.: 587 (1956-79), 804 (1982-89)
- Urb/Rur Dev.: 205 (1956-79), 59 (1982-89)
- Other Dev.: 190 (1956-79), 102 (1982-89)
- Ponds: 394 (1956-79), 414 (1982-89)
- Res./Lake: 17 (1956-79), 138 (1982-89)

Legend: 1956-79, 1982-89

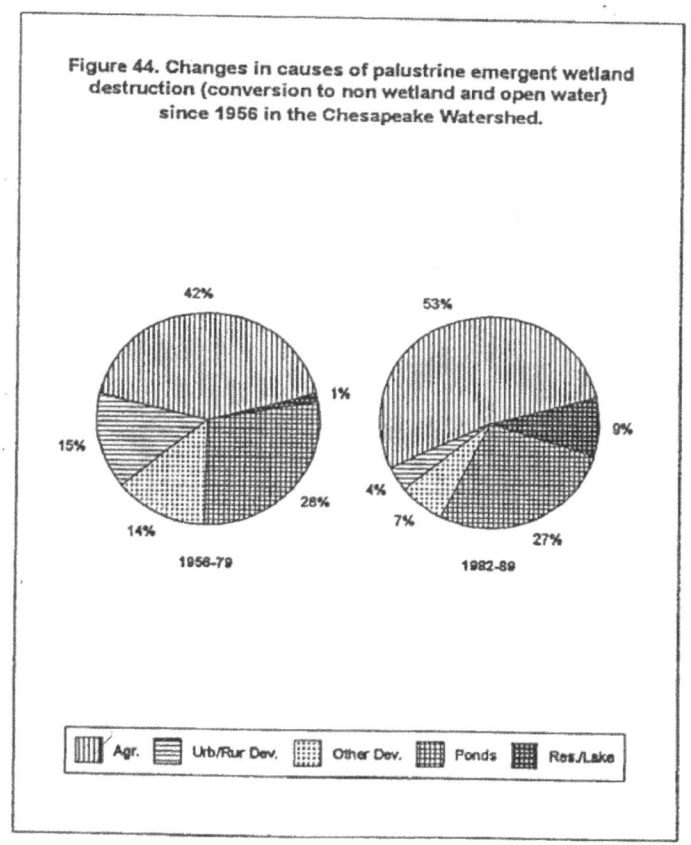

Figure 44. Changes in causes of palustrine emergent wetland destruction (conversion to non wetland and open water) since 1956 in the Chesapeake Watershed.

1956-79: 42%, 1%, 26%, 14%, 15%
1982-89: 53%, 9%, 27%, 7%, 4%

Legend: Agr., Urb/Rur Dev., Other Dev., Ponds, Res./Lake

61

CONCLUSIONS AND RECOMMENDATIONS

This report represents the first wetland status and trends study designed exclusively for the Chesapeake Watershed. As such, it provides the most up-to-date and accurate information on the status and trends of wetlands in the Watershed. This type of study provides, in large part, a comprehensive overview of the cumulative recent impacts of agriculture, urban development, impoundment construction, timber harvest, beaver influences, and other factors on wetlands and will be useful for evaluating current policies affecting wetlands. These results will also prove invaluable to regulatory agencies, natural resource managers and planners, environmental organizations, and the general public in making future land use decisions and in addressing the Watershed's major wetland problems. While this report documents recent trends in the extent of wetlands, it does not address changes in the quality of the remaining wetlands. Today, wetlands are subjected to a multitude of perturbations that reduce their quality. Water pollution from urban, agricultural, and industrial sources, increased sedimentation and erosion related to changing land uses, channelization and ditching projects, reduced freshwater inflows, ground-water withdrawals, human-induced changes in naturally vegetated buffers around wetlands, and various forms of urban encroachment are among many factors adversely impacting the quality of wetlands.

Significant gains in freshwater ponds and substantial losses of vegetated wetlands continue to take place in the Watershed. The importance of the gain in pond acreage to fish and wildlife species has not been assessed and is still subject to much discussion. Some of the additional acreage seems to succeed into palustrine emergent wetlands which should have at least some value for wetland wildlife, depending on variables such as adjacent land use, wetland size, plant community structure, and adjacent natural buffers. By contrast, the continued losses of naturally occurring estuarine marshes and forests and palustrine vegetated wetlands represent losses of valuable fish and wildlife habitats and losses of the many other environmental quality and socio-economic values provided free-of-charge to society by wetlands. Moreover, the significance of the vegetated wetland losses is not simply reflected by the acreages alone, since prior to the study period, many wetlands had already been destroyed, making the remaining wetlands more important and future losses more serious.

While coastal wetlands received much better protection in the 1980s than before, palustrine vegetated wetlands remain in jeopardy. Loss rates of these wetlands continued at high levels in the 1980s despite the existence of Federal wetland regulations. All palustrine vegetated wetland types exhibited net losses: forested (net loss of over 14,000 acres), scrub-shrub (nearly 1,000 acres), and emergent (over 4,000). Actual destruction of existing wetlands was greater than reflected by the net numbers (see Table 12).

From concurrent wetland trends studies conducted in specific areas within the Chesapeake Watershed (see Appendix B for highlights), seasonally saturated and temporarily flooded forested wetlands are being destroyed at higher rates than other palustrine forests. These wetlands have received little or no protection probably for three main reasons: (1) most of these wetlands are delineated as "nonjurisdictional uplands" following a strict interpretation of the 1987 Corps manual for wetland delineation (Jennings, et al. 1993), (2) the functions and values of these wetlands are not well understood, and (3) the widely held belief that wetter wetlands are generically better or more valuable than drier types.

The 1987 Corps manual typically requires that areas considered as regulatory wetlands must have positive indicators of three parameters: hydrophytic vegetation, hydric soils, and wetland hydrology (Environmental Laboratory 1987). The hydrology indicators listed in the manual are surface water indicators, except for the observation of saturation within 12 inches of the soil surface.[2] Seasonally saturated and temporarily flooded wetlands are usually wettest during the winter and are locally called "winter wet woods". The requirement for wetness for 5.0 - 12.5 percent of the growing season as specified in the manual also prevents these wetlands from being identified as regulated wetlands (Tiner 1993a, 1993b). Moreover, the definition of "growing season" used to evaluate the wetland hydrology parameter (e.g., minimum wetness requirement) can further limit the extent of these wetlands. For example, using the frost-free period yields the shortest "growing season", while using the period above biologic zero in soil or the biologically active period would increase the "growing season" to the one that native wetland plants are responding to.

Although the functions of seasonally saturated forested wetlands are not well understood, there is enough information to support at least some level of regulation or enhance existing regulatory efforts. In January 1992, a workshop focusing on these wetlands presented considerable information on their functions and values and some of the papers have been published in a workshop proceedings (Eckles, et al. 1992) and in a special edition of Wetlands (Volume 13, Number 2). Furthermore, studies in Florida suggest that isolated wetlands in low relief landscapes help reduce peak floods and increase ground-water levels (Brown and Sullivan 1988). This is probably also true for seasonally saturated and temporarily flooded wetlands on the Coastal Plain in the Chesapeake Watershed. The above studies should provide enough evidence of important functions and values to support increased regulations of alterations to these wetlands. If more information is required, the government should support the needed research to answer the pertinent questions.

Recommendations

The following recommendations are offered to help improve the status of wetlands in the Chesapeake Watershed. Some of the suggestions are specific to the Watershed, while most are of a general nature applicable to many areas in the eastern U.S. and elsewhere. They include both regulatory and nonregulatory initiatives, since regulatory programs alone cannot solve wetland-land use conflicts.

1. Develop and adopt strategies to increase protection of palustrine vegetated wetlands, especially for seasonally saturated and temporarily flooded wetlands

---

[2]Recent Corps guidance has expanded the list of indicators to permit use of oxidized rhizospheres, the FAC neutral test, and water table data from published soil surveys (verify hydric soil in the field). This will help identify some, but not all of these seasonally saturated wetlands.

and isolated wetlands on the Coastal Plain and for Virginia and Delaware. Such strategies must address agricultural uses of wetlands, since such activities have remained to be major causes of wetland losses in the Watershed. Other activities that need to be included in these strategies are aquaculture, regulated shooting areas, and forestry practices in wetlands. These strategies must incorporate both regulatory and nonregulatory approaches to wetland – conservation and management.

2. Interpret the regulatory definition of wetland in a scientifically sound manner and use science-based techniques to identify these wetlands on the ground. Use policy to regulate uses of wetlands and not to define what a wetland is. It is more efficient and effective to change policy to meet current needs than to try to change established scientific principles and practices to satisfy a public policy need.

3. In southeastern Virginia where palustrine vegetated wetlands are disappearing at an alarming rate, it may be advisable to establish an intergovernmental committee (Federal, state, and local) to develop a regional strategy for reducing wetland losses while pursuing realistic economic growth. This is perhaps the greatest challenge for similar "wetland loss hotspots" in the country. It may require developing innovative tax incentives and wetland acquisition initiatives and establishing realistic land use options and growth/development limits that maintain and enhance existing environmental quality. The 1988 report entitled "Population Growth and Development in the Chesapeake Bay Watershed to the Year 2020" provides insight into the problems and the vision of how this may be accomplished. This report offers many specific recommendations that should be implemented to maintain a high quality environment in the Watershed. This recommendation is also applicable to other wetland loss hotspots.

4. Eliminate government-sponsored wetland channelization and ditching programs and seek other more environmentally acceptable means of reducing flood damages, e.g., natural valley storage approach. Studies have shown that complete drainage of wetlands eliminates all their beneficial effects on water quality and directly contributes to flooding problems (Lee, et al. 1975, among others).

5. Locate stormwater basins and agricultural sediment ponds outside of wetlands and of streams. With increasing urban development, stream flows increase leading to accelerated erosion of streambanks and streambeds. Proper location of these basins should minimize wetland and stream impacts.

6. Increase wetland acquisition to preserve functions of existing wetland systems. Identify large tracts of remaining wetlands and strive to connect them together, thereby linking presently isolated tracts into an interconnected network of

wetlands. This effort attempts to minimize wetland fragmentation for improved wildlife habitat and should enhance other wetland functions as well.

7. Identify wetland landscapes in need of restoration and initiate large-scale restoration efforts to restore ecosystem functions.

8. Develop measures and programs to maintain and establish vegetated buffers around wetlands and along waterbodies. This could produce significant water quality benefits and enhance fish and wildlife habitat values.

9. Instead of wetland trend studies, develop and initiate monitoring programs to provide more real-time assessment of wetlands for analyzing and modifying current policies before too much wetland destruction occurs.

10. Conduct research to increase our knowledge of the hydrology and functions of seasonally saturated wetlands and isolated temporarily flooded wetlands on the Coastal Plain.

11. Develop outreach programs to encourage private landowners to protect their wetlands and/or to minimize wetland alteration during activities such as timber harvest.

12. Continue to increase public education efforts. A well informed public will likely select environmentally sound approaches to land use in the future.

Wetlands are the vital link between land and water. As such, they help improve water quality, temporarily store water to prevent downstream flooding, stabilize shorelines, and provide numerous other functions that benefit society. If we are to continue to receive these benefits, action must be taken to reverse the trends observed in the 1980s and earlier. We must continue our efforts to conserve estuarine wetlands which significantly slowed the losses of these wetlands. Our attention must now focus on the nontidal palustrine wetlands which remain under heavy threat for development. The living resources of Chesapeake Bay also depend on the welfare of these wetlands which help filter out excess nutrients, sediments, and other pollutants, thereby preventing these potentially deleterious materials from reaching the Bay. We must strengthen wetland protection and initiate wetland restoration efforts to improve the quality of the Bay for its living resources, for ourselves, and for future generations. Our quality of life is largely dependent on the abundance and condition of our natural resources. The significance of our land and water resources should not be underestimated. Based on the past experiences of other civilizations, how we manage our natural environment will largely determine the fate of our society.

REFERENCES

Brown, M.T. and M.F. Sullivan. 1988. Chapter 11. The value of wetlands in low relief landscapes. In: D.D. Hook and others (eds.). The Ecology and Management of Wetlands. Volume 1: Ecology of Wetlands. Timber Press, Portland, OR. pp. 133 - 145.

Cowardin, L.M., V. Carter, F.C. Golet, and E.T. LaRoe. 1979. Classification of Wetlands and Deepwater Habitats of the United States. U.S. Fish and Wildlife Service, Washington, DC. FWS/OBS-79/31. 103 pp.

Dahl, T.E., and C. Johnson. 1991. Wetlands Status and Trends in the Conterminous United States, Mid-1970s to Mid-1980s. U.S. Department of the Interior, Fish and Wildlife Service, Washington, DC. 28 pp.

Eckles, S.D., A. Jennings, A. Spingarn, and C. Wienhold (eds). 1992. Proceedings of a Workshop on Saturated Forested Wetlands in the Mid-Atlantic Region: The State of the Science.

Environmental Laboratory. 1987. Corps Wetlands Delineation Manual. U.S. Army Corps of Engineers, Waterways Expt. Station, Vicksburg, MS. Technical report Y-87-1, 100 pp. plus appendices.

Environmental Laboratory. 1987. Corps of Engineers Wetlands Delineation Manual. U.S. Army Corps of Engineers, Vicksburg, MS. Tech. Rept. Y-87-1.

Environmental Opinion Study, Inc. 1991. Survey of American Voters: Attitudes Toward the Environment. (Results of May 26, 1991 poll) Washington, DC. 34 pp.

Federal Interagency Committee for Wetland Delineation. 1989. Federal Manual for Identifying and Delineating Jurisdictional Wetlands. U.S. Army Corps of Engineers, U.S. Environmental Protection Agency, U.S. Fish and Wildlife Service, and U.S.D.A. Soil Conservation Service, Washington, DC. Cooperative technical publication, 76 pp. plus appendices.

Fenneman, N.M. 1928. Physical Divisions of the United States. Annals of the Association of American Geographers 18: 261-353.

Frayer, W.E., T.J. Monahan, D.C. Bowden, and F.A. Graybill. 1983. Status and Trends of Wetlands and Deepwater Habitats in the Conterminous United States, 1950's to 1970's. Dept. of Forest and Wood Sciences, Colorado State Univ., Ft. Collins. 32 pp.

Frayer, W.E. 1991. Status and Trends of Wetlands and Deepwater Habitats in the Conterminous United States, 1970s to 1980s. Michigan Technological University, School of Forestry and Wood Products, Holton, MI. 31 pp.

Hammond, E.H. 1970. Physical subdivisions of the United States. In: National Atlas of the United States. U.S. Geological Survey, Washington, DC. 417 pp.

Harris, L. 1982. A Survey of American Attitudes Toward Water Pollution. Prepared for the Natural Resources Council of America. December 15, 1982.

Jennings, A., D. Eckles, A. Spingarn, C. Wienhold, and A. Bartuska. 1993. Saturated forested wetlands. National Wetlands Newsletter 15(4): 7 - 9.

Lee, G.F., E. Bentley, and R. Amundson. 1975. Effects of marshes on water quality. In: A.D. Hasler (editor). Coupling of Land and Water Systems. Springer-Verlag, New York. pp. 105-127.

Schubel, J.R. 1986. The Life and Death of the Chesapeake Bay. University of Maryland, College Park. Maryland Sea Grant Publication UM-SG-MP-86-01. 45 pp.

The Year 2020 Panel. 1988. Population Growth and Development in the Chesapeake Bay Watershed to the Year 2020. Printed by the U.S. Environmental Protection Agency for the Chesapeake Bay Program, Annapolis, MD. 52 pp. plus appendices.

Tiner, R.W., Jr. 1984. Wetlands of the United States: Current Status and Recent Trends. U.S. Fish and Wildlife Serv., National Wetlands Inventory, Washington, D.C. 59 pp.

Tiner, R.W., Jr. 1985. Wetlands of Delaware. U.S. Fish and Wildlife Serv., National Wetlands Inventory, Newton Corner, MA and Delaware Dept. of Nat. Res. and Env'tal Control, Wetlands Section. Dover, DE. Cooperative publication. 77 pp.

Tiner, R.W. 1987. Mid-Atlantic Wetlands: A Disappearing Natural Treasure. U.S. Fish and Wildlife Service, Region 5, Newton Corner, MA and U.S. Environmental Protection Agency, Region III, Philadelphia, PA. 28 pp.

Tiner, R.W. 1993a. Field recognition and delineation of wetlands. Chapter 5. In: M.S. Dennison and J.F. Berry (eds.). Wetlands: Guide to Science, Law, and Technology. Noyes Publications, Park Ridge, NJ. pp. 153 - 198.

Tiner, R.W. 1993b. Problem wetlands for delineation. Chapter 6. In: M.S. Dennison, and J.F. Berry (editors). Wetlands: Guide to Science, Law, and Technology. Noyes Publications, Park Ridge, NJ. pp. 199 - 212.

Tiner, R.W. 1994. Recent Wetland Status and Trends in the Chesapeake Watershed (1982 to 1989): Executive Summary Report. Prepared by the U.S. Fish and Wildlife Service, Region 5, Hadley, MA, for the Chesapeake Bay Program, Annapolis, MD. 12 pp.

Tiner, R.W. and J.T. Finn. 1986. Status and Recent Trends of Wetland in Five Mid-Atlantic States: Delaware, Maryland, Pennsylvania, Virginia, and West Virginia. U.S. Fish and Wildlife Service, Region 5, Newton Corner, MA and U.S. Environmental

Protection Agency, Region III, Philadelphia, PA. Cooperative technical publication. 40 pp.

Tiner, R.W. and D.B. Foulis. 1994. Wetland Trends in Selected Areas of the Norfolk/Hampton Region of Virginia (1982 to 1989-90). U.S. Fish and Wildlife Service, Hadley, MA. Ecological Services report R5-93/16. 18 pp.

Wolfe, P.E. 1977. The Geology and Landscapes of New Jersey. Crane, Rewsak, and Co., Inc. 351 pp.

GLOSSARY

For the convenience of the reader, several terms are defined below. The definition emphasizes the use of these terms in respect to the wetland trends analysis study.

Agriculture. Activities related to farming and grazing, including row crop production, pastures, orchards, and vineyards, and associated farm buildings (e.g., chicken coops, silos, and barns). Crops may be produced for human consumption, livestock, or wildlife game species (e.g., waterfowl at regulated shooting areas).

Change, wetland. An alteration in the condition of a wetland, may involve simply a change in the type of wetland, e.g., from emergent wetland to scrub-shrub wetland, or a change from wetland to nonwetland due to natural events or human activities (e.g., filling).

Conversion, wetland. Same as definition of wetland change, but usually emphasizes changes due to human activities.

Deepwater habitat. An open waterbody, in freshwater deeper than 6.6 feet at mean low water and in marine and estuarine areas, extends below the mean low spring tide level, includes lakes, reservoirs, rivers, estuarine embayments, and the ocean.

Destroyed wetland. Wetland that is converted to open water habitats (e.g., pond or reservoir) or to dryland (nonwetland), typically due to human activities.

Estuarine wetlands. Tidally-influenced salt and brackish marshes and swamps where salinity from ocean-derived salts is usually above 0.5 parts per thousand.

Gain, wetland. The increase in wetland acreage of a given type over time. A net gain reflects the situation where gains in a particular wetland type exceed losses in that type during a specific period of time (e.g., 1982 to 1989).

Impoundment. A diked wetland or waterbody; purpose of diking may be to keep water in or to keep water out (e.g., salt water), includes, but is not limited to, aquaculture ponds and waterfowl ponds.

Lake. A nontidal open waterbody usually greater than 20 acres in size, includes natural lakes and man-made lakes.

Loss, wetland. The decrease in wetland acreage of a given type over time. Losses of a given wetland type, therefore, include changes in wetland type and conversions to open waterbodies and to dryland (nonwetlands). A net loss reflects the situation where losses in a particular wetland type exceed gains in that type during a specific period of time (e.g., 1982 to 1989).

Nontidal wetland. A typically freshwater wetland that is beyond the influence of the ocean-driven tides.

Nonwetland. Lands that are not subject to wetland hydrology; equivalent to drylands or uplands, but also includes effectively drained former wetlands.

Palustrine wetlands. Freshwater marshes, swamps, and bogs that are mostly nontidal, but also includes freshwater tidal marshes and swamps where salinity from ocean-derived salts is less than 0.5 parts per thousand.

Pond. A shallow, fresh waterbody less than 20 acres in size and usually less than 6.6 feet deep at mean annual low water, includes both natural and man-made ponds.

Regulated shooting area. Private hunting areas in Maryland stocked with mostly pen-raised mallards; hunting is regulated by Maryland Department of Natural Resources; many of these areas involved wetland alterations, e.g., converting palustrine forests to cropland or ponds.

Reservoir. A large, deep waterbody created by damming a natural valley to provide public drinking water.

Status, wetland. As used in this report, quantitative measure of the condition of a particular wetland type, usually expressed in acres.

Tidal wetland. Marshes and swamps whose water levels rise and fall with the tides, includes both estuarine (saltwater) wetlands and tidal palustrine (freshwater) wetlands.

Trend, wetland. As used in this report, the quantitative changes that take place in wetlands of a given type over type, i.e., changes in acreage.

Wetland. Lands transitional between terrestrial and aquatic systems where the water table is usually at or near the surface or the land is covered by shallow water; such lands must have one or more of the following attributes: (1) at least periodically supports predominantly hydrophytes, (2) substrate is predominantly undrained (not effectively drained) hydric soils, and (3) nonsoil substrate that is saturated with water or covered by shallow water at some time during the growing season of each year.

Wetland trend analysis study. A scientific examination of the acreage changes that occur in wetlands in a given geographic region over time. In this study, the trends are quantitative and not qualitative.

APPENDIX A

List of Wetland Trends Reports for Specific Geographic Areas
Within the Chesapeake Watershed

Tiner, R.W. and D.B. Foulis. 1993. Wetland Status and Trends in Selected Areas of Maryland's Piedmont Region (1980-81 to 1988-89). U.S. Fish and Wildlife Service, Hadley, MA. Ecological Services report R5-93/03. 12 pp.

Tiner, R.W. and D.B. Foulis. 1993. Wetland Status and Trends in Selected Areas of Maryland's Fall Zone (1981-82 to 1988-89). U.S. Fish and Wildlife Service, Hadley, MA. Ecological Services report R5-93/04. 12 pp.

Tiner, R.W. and D.B. Foulis. 1993. Wetland Trends in Selected Areas of the Western Shore Region of Maryland (1981 to 1988). U.S. Fish and Wildlife Service, Hadley, MA. Ecological Services report R5-93/05. 13 pp.

Tiner, R.W. and D.B. Foulis. 1993. Wetland Trends for the North East Quadrangle in Maryland (1981 to 1988). U.S. Fish and Wildlife Service, Hadley, MA. Ecological Services report R5-93/06. 9 pp.

Tiner, R.W. and D.B. Foulis. 1993. Wetland Trends for the Kent Island and Queenstown Quadrangles in Eastern Maryland (1982 to 1989). U.S. Fish and Wildlife Service, Hadley, MA. Ecological Services report R5-93/07. 11 pp.

Tiner, R.W. and D.B. Foulis. 1993. Wetland Trends for the DuBois and Falls Creek Quadrangles in Pennsylvania (1983 to 1988). U.S. Fish and Wildlife Service, Hadley, MA. Ecological Services report R5-93/08. 10 pp.

Tiner, R.W. and D.B. Foulis. 1993. Wetland Trends in the Williamsport Area of Pennsylvania (1977 to 1988/90). U.S. Fish and Wildlife Service, Hadley, MA. Ecological Services report R5-93/09. 11 pp.

Tiner, R.W. and D.B. Foulis. 1993. Wetland Trends for the Hazelton Quadrangle in Pennsylvania (1981 to 1987). U.S. Fish and Wildlife Service, Hadley, MA. Ecological Services report R5-93/10. 10 pp.

Tiner, R.W. and D.B. Foulis. 1993. Wetland Trends in Selected Areas of the Greater Harrisburg Region of Pennsylvania (1983-84 to 1987-88). U.S. Fish and Wildlife Service, Hadley, MA. Ecological Services report R5-93/11. 11 pp.

Tiner, R.W., D.B. Foulis, and T.W. Nuerminger. 1994. Wetland Trends for Selected Areas of the Northeast Glaciated Region of Pennsylvania (1981-82 to 1987-88). U.S. Fish and Wildlife Service, Hadley, MA. Ecological Services report R5-93/12. 13 pp.

Tiner, R.W. and D.B. Foulis. 1994. Wetland Trends for Selected Areas of Dorchester County, Maryland and Vicinity (1981-82 to 1988-89). U.S. Fish and Wildlife Service, Hadley, MA. Ecological Services report R5-93/14. 17 pp.

Tiner, R.W. and D.B. Foulis. 1994. Wetland Trends for Selected Areas of the Lower Eastern Shore of the Delmarva Peninsula (1982 to 1988-89). U.S. Fish and Wildlife Service, Hadley, MA. Ecological Services report R5-93/15. 12 pp.

Tiner, R.W. and D.B. Foulis. 1994. Wetland Trends in Selected Areas of the Norfolk/Hampton Region of Virginia (1982 to 1989-90). U.S. Fish and Wildlife Service, Hadley, MA. Ecological Services report R5-93/16. 18 pp.

Tiner, R.W. and D.B. Foulis. 1994. Wetland Trends for Selected Areas in Northern Virginia (1980-81 to 1988/91). U.S. Fish and Wildlife Service, Hadley, MA. Ecological Services report R5-93/17. 13 pp.

Tiner, R.W. and D.B. Foulis. 1994. Wetland Trends for Selected Areas of the Chickahominy River Watershed of Virginia (1982/84 to 1989-90). U.S. Fish and Wildlife Service, Hadley, MA. Ecological Services report R5-93/18. 15 pp.

APPENDIX B

Highlights of Detailed Wetland Trends Studies for Specific
Geographic Areas in Virginia, Maryland, and Pennsylvania

WETLAND TRENDS STUDY HIGHLIGHTS - **VIRGINIA**

STUDY AREA:

Norfolk-Hampton region - 12 Quads (Bowers Hill, Deep Creek, Fentress, Hampton, Kempsville, Mulberry Island, Newport News North, Norfolk South, Poquoson East, Poquoson West, Princess Anne, and Yorktown)

STUDY PERIOD: 1982 to 1989/90

MAJOR FINDINGS:

1. Changes in Vegetated Wetlands:

Wetland Type	Converted to Upland (acres)	Changed to Other PVEG Types (acres)	Changed to Pond/Deepwater (acres)
E2EM	34.13	2.02	1.43/8.73
E2SS	2.29	.00	0/0.51
PEM	382.62	568.10	16.42/2.42
PFO	3,934.02	2,050.22	113.88/61.27
PSS	493.76	1,666.33	9.43/0
TOTAL	4,846.82	4,286.47	141.16/72.93

2. Causes of Palustrine Vegetated Wetland Loss to Upland:

Housing (2,050.85 acres), Agriculture (1,202.21), Sanitary Land Fill (397.03), Resort Development (266.77), Ditching (243.04), Roads and Highways (131.44), Commercial Development (126.55), Unknown (89.78), Canals (72.79), Sand and Gravel Pits (67.62), Industrial Development (45.12), and Other (120.18).

3. Type Most Converted to Upland:

PFO, Seasonally Saturated (2,182.09 acres); PFO, Temporarily Flooded (807.97 acres)

4. Gains in PVEG Wetlands from Upland:

90.02 acres (mostly PEM, 60.43 acres)

5. New Pond Acreage Created:

756.31 (615.15 from Upland; 141.16 from Wetland)

WETLAND TRENDS STUDY HIGHLIGHTS - **VIRGINIA**

STUDY AREA:

Chickahominy River area - 7 Quads (Norge, Providence Forge, Richmond, Roxbury, Seven Pines, Walkers, and Yellow Tavern)

STUDY PERIOD: 1982/84 to 1989/90

MAJOR FINDINGS:

1. Changes in Vegetated Wetlands:

Wetland Type	Converted to Upland (acres)	Changed to Other PVEG Types (acres)	Changed to Pond/Deepwater (acres)
PEM	2.52	25.04	19.26/18.14
PFO	86.59	240.25	73.05/11.10
PSS	12.90	18.89	38.15/22.13
TOTAL	102.01	284.18	130.46/51.37

2. Causes of Palustrine Vegetated Wetland Loss to Upland:

Sand and Gravel Pits (35.92 acres), Roads (20.71), Ditching (12.08), Housing (8.22), Resort Development (5.55), Airport (2.78), Commercial Development (2.52), Agriculture (1.19), and Unknown (13.04).

3. Type Most Converted to Upland:

PFO, Seasonally Flooded/Saturated (55.31 acres)

4. Gains in PVEG Wetlands from Upland:

16.96 acres (PSS - 10.61 and PEM - 6.35)

5. New Pond Acreage Created:

193.31 (62.85 from Upland; 130.46 from Wetland)

WETLAND TRENDS STUDY HIGHLIGHTS - **VIRGINIA**

STUDY AREA:

Northern Virginia - 6 Quads (Arcola, Fairfax, Fredericksburg, Herndon, Manassas, and Vienna)

STUDY PERIOD: 1980/81 to 1988/91

MAJOR FINDINGS:

1.   Changes in Vegetated Wetlands:

Wetland Type	Converted to Upland (acres)	Changed to Other PVEG Types (acres)	Changed to Pond/Deepwater (acres)
PAB	1.22	.00	.00
PEM	29.51	13.72	21.42*
PFO	80.24	52.37	16.83
PSS	16.05	14.82	10.04
TOTAL	127.02	80.91	48.29

*Includes 6.12 acres converted to lakes/reservoirs

2.   Causes of Palustrine Vegetated Wetland Loss to Upland:

Commercial Development (41.54 acres), Housing (27.77), Roads/Highways (27.33), Airports (6.23), Industrial Development (5.66), Agriculture (4.56), Ditching (3.24), Unknown (2.74), Transmission Line Corridors (2.65), Sand and Gravel Pits (2.14), Public Facilities (2.12), Recreational Facilities (0.86), and Public Sewer Facilities (0.18).

3.   Type Most Converted to Upland:

PFO, Seasonally Flooded (49.20 acres)

4.   Gains in PVEG Wetlands from Upland:

12.53 acres

5.   New Pond Acreage Created:

167.68 (125.51 from Upland; 42.17 from Wetland)

WETLAND TRENDS STUDY HIGHLIGHTS - **MARYLAND**

STUDY AREA:

Dorchester County area - 6 Quads (Preston, Church Creek, Cambridge, Golden Hill, Blackwater River, and Wingate)

STUDY PERIOD: 1981/82 to 1988/89

MAJOR FINDINGS:

1. Changes in Palustrine Vegetated Wetlands:

Wetland Type	Converted to Upland (acres)	Changed to Other PVEG Types (acres)	Changed to Pond/Deepwater (acres)
PEM	63.13	17.31	38.01
PFO	607.52	2,054.87	63.47
PSS	111.40	.00	3.77
TOTAL	782.05	2,072.18*	105.25

*Most of the changes reflect timber harvest and subsequent successional patterns in the plant communities.

2. Causes of Palustrine Vegetated Wetland Loss to Upland:

Agriculture including cropland associated with regulated shooting areas and farmed wetland (711.05), Roads (18.22), Dams for Farm Ponds (11.49), Housing and Commercial Development (14.5), and Other (26.79).

3. Type Most Converted to Upland:

PFO, Temporarily Flooded/Seasonally Saturated (435.06 acres)

4. New Pond Acreage Created:

174.3 (69.05 from Upland; 105.25 from Wetland)

5. Changes in Estuarine Vegetated (EVEG) Wetlands:

Wetland Type	Converted to Upland (acres)	Changed to Other EVEG Types (acres)	Changed to Flats (acres)
E2EM	19.76	6.84	3.72
E2FO	75.31	169.19	.00
E2SS	1.49	.00	.00
TOTAL	96.56	176.03	3.72

6. Causes of EVEG Lost to Upland:

Agriculture including cropland associated with regulated shooting areas (73.77 acres), Unknown (6.77), Wildlife Management (6.43), Dredged Spoil Disposal (4.8), Marina (3.73), and Other (1.1).

7. Changes in EVEG Due to Sea Level Rise and Coastal Erosion:

Estuarine Forests to Dead Forests (352.71), Stressed Estuarine Forests (Partly Dead Timber) (208.92), Estuarine Forests to Salt Marsh (29.23), Salt Marsh to Open Water (16.58), and Gain in Estuarine Forests from Palustrine Forests (72.26).

WETLAND TRENDS STUDY HIGHLIGHTS - **MARYLAND**

STUDY AREA:

Lower Eastern Shore - 5 Quads (Delmar, Pittsville, Salisbury, Wango, and Princess Anne)

STUDY PERIOD: 1982 to 1988/89

MAJOR FINDINGS:

1. Changes in Vegetated Wetlands:

Wetland Type	Converted to Upland (acres)	Changed to Other PVEG Types (acres)	Changed to Pond/Deepwater (acres)
PEM	11.55	579.11	.00
PFO	173.53	1,678.22	2.19
PSS	2.76	481.83	.00
TOTAL	187.84	2,739.16*	2.19

*2,606.97 acres reflect timber harvest and subsequent successional patterns in the plant communities.

2. Causes of Palustrine Vegetated Wetland Loss to Upland:

Agriculture (106.08 acres), Ditching (51.89), Public Facilities (13.96), Housing (9.20) and Other (6.71).

3. Type Most Converted to Upland:

PFO, Temporarily Flooded (154.0 acres)

4. Gains in PVEG Wetlands from Upland:

1.7 acres

5. New Pond Acreage Created:

47.74 (45.55 from Upland; 2.19 from Wetland)

WETLAND TRENDS STUDY HIGHLIGHTS - **MARYLAND**

STUDY AREA:

Western Shore - 8 Quads (Odenton, Deale, Upper Marlboro, Brandywine, Piscataway, Hughesville, La Plata, and Popes Creek).

STUDY PERIOD: 1981 to 1988

MAJOR FINDINGS:

1. Changes in Vegetated Wetlands:

Wetland Type	Converted to Upland (acres)	Changed to Other PVEG Types (acres)	Changed to Pond/Deepwater (acres)
E2EM	0.24	.00	.00
PEM	21.91	34.14	3.52
PFO	115.42	52.74	22.40
PSS	5.83	5.87	8.74
TOTAL	143.16	92.75	34.66

2. Causes of Vegetated Wetland Loss to Upland:

    Housing (51.28 acres), Unknown (31.83), Sand and Gravel Pits (22.78), Commercial Development (17.40), Road Construction (11.51), Agriculture (5.78), and Government Installation (2.82).

3. Type Most Converted to Upland:

    PFO, Temporarily Flooded (81.31 acres)

4. Gains in PVEG Wetlands from Upland:

    28.87 acres

5. New Pond Acreage Created:

    167.19 (132.53 from Upland; 34.66 from Wetland)

WETLAND TRENDS STUDY HIGHLIGHTS - **MARYLAND**

STUDY AREA:

Kent Island area - 2 Quads (Kent Island and Queenstown).

STUDY PERIOD: 1982 to 1989

MAJOR FINDINGS:

1.   Changes in Vegetated Wetlands:

Wetland Type	Converted to Upland (acres)	Changed to Other PVEG Types (acres)	Changed to Pond/Deepwater (acres)
E2EM	60.81	2.80	5.41
E2SS	3.73	.00	.00
PEM	3.67	3.50	.00
PFO	11.84	0.91	.00
PSS	7.93	.00	.00
TOTAL	87.98	7.21	5.41

2.   Causes of Vegetated Wetland Loss to Upland:

Housing (43.34 acres), Agriculture (13.32), Commercial Development (12.72), Roads/Highways (10.02), Marina (6.68), Pond Dams (1.17), and Airport (0.73).

3.   Type Most Converted to Upland:

E2EM (60.81 acres)

4.   Gains in PVEG Wetlands from Upland:

3.01 acres

5.   New Pond Acreage Created:

51.98 (44.77 from Upland; 7.21 from Wetland)

WETLAND TRENDS STUDY HIGHLIGHTS - MARYLAND

STUDY AREA:

North East Quadrangle

STUDY PERIOD: 1981 to 1988

MAJOR FINDINGS:

1. Changes in Vegetated Wetlands:

Wetland Type	Converted to Upland (acres)	Changed to Other PVEG Types (acres)
PEM	0.61	1.33
PFO	.00	3.93
PSS	.00	5.16
TOTAL	0.61	10.42

2. Causes of Palustrine Vegetated Wetland Loss to Upland:

    Commercial/Business Development (0.61 acres)

3. Gains in PVEG Wetlands from Upland:

    5.21 acres

4. New Pond Acreage Created:

    8.89 (7.72 from Upland; 1.17 from Wetland)

WETLAND TRENDS STUDY HIGHLIGHTS - **MARYLAND**

STUDY AREA:

Fall Zone - 2 Quads (Relay and White Marsh)

STUDY PERIOD: 1981/82 to 1988/89

MAJOR FINDINGS:

1. Changes in Vegetated Wetlands:

Wetland Type	Converted to Upland (acres)	Changed to Other PVEG Types (acres)
PEM	0.80	.00
PFO	13.06	7.72
PSS	2.25	4.38
TOTAL	16.11	12.10

2. Causes of Palustrine Vegetated Wetland Loss to Upland:

   Housing (8.57 acres), Roads/Highways (6.75), Unknown (0.44) and Sand and Gravel Pits (0.35).

3. Type Most Converted to Upland:

   PFO, Temporarily Flooded (9.57 acres)

4. New Pond Acreage Created:

   23.26 (20.71 from Upland; 2.55 from Wetland)

WETLAND TRENDS STUDY HIGHLIGHTS - **MARYLAND**

STUDY AREA:

Piedmont region - 6 Quads (Buckeystown, Kensington, Libertytown, Rockville, Urbana, and Walkersville).

STUDY PERIOD: 1980/81 to 1988/89

MAJOR FINDINGS:

1. Changes in Vegetated Wetlands:

Wetland Type	Converted to Upland (acres)	Changed to Other PVEG Types (acres)	Changed to Pond/Deepwater (acres)
PEM	56.56	33.47	7.54
PFO	28.27	0.82	1.65
PSS	3.62	.00	0.53
TOTAL	88.45	34.29	9.72

2. Causes of Palustrine Vegetated Wetland Loss to Upland:

Agriculture (44.16 acres), Roads/Highways (28.76), Housing (9.14), Unknown (2.71), Ditching (2.09), and Commercial/Industrial Development (1.59).

3. Types Most Converted to Upland:

PEM, Temporarily Flooded (32.81 acres) and PFO, Temporarily Flooded (21.87 acres)

4. Gains in PVEG Wetlands from Upland:

0.71 acres

5. New Pond Acreage Created:

84.94 (75.22 from Upland; 9.72 from Wetland)

WETLAND TRENDS STUDY HIGHLIGHTS - PENNSYLVANIA

STUDY AREA:

Northeast Glaciated region - 13 Quads (Center Moreland, Dalton, Factoryville, Great Bend, Harford, Lawton, Montrose East, Montrose West, Ransom, Sayre, Towanda, Tunkhannock, and Ulster).

STUDY PERIOD: 1981/82 to 1987/88

MAJOR FINDINGS:

1. Changes in Vegetated Wetlands:

Wetland Type	Converted to Upland (acres)	Changed to Other PVEG Types (acres)	Changed to Pond (acres)
PEM	38.47	35.27	116.68
PFO	6.59	33.31	8.97
PSS	12.75	49.12	34.21
TOTAL	57.81	117.70	159.86*

*An additional 11 acres were converted to lakes/reservoirs.

2. Causes of Palustrine Vegetated Wetland Loss to Upland:

Agriculture (30.01 acres), Housing (12.73), Industrial Development (4.65), Aquaculture (3.24), Recreational Facilities (2.89), Commercial Development (2.27), Unknown (1.39), and Dams for Ponds (0.63).

3. Type Most Converted to Upland:

PEM, Seasonally Flooded/Saturated (28.60 acres)

4. Gains in PVEG Wetlands from Upland:

18.94 acres

5. New Pond Acreage Created:

268.89 (109.03 from Upland; 159.86 from Wetland)

WETLAND TRENDS STUDY HIGHLIGHTS - **PENNSYLVANIA**

STUDY AREA:

Greater Harrisburg - 13 Quads (Landisburg, Newport, Shermans Dale, Carlisle, Duncannon, Halifax, Harrisburg East, Middleton, York Haven, Columbia West, Columbia East, Manheim, and Terre Hill).

STUDY PERIOD: 1983/84 to 1987/88

MAJOR FINDINGS:

1. Changes in Vegetated Wetlands:

Wetland Type	Converted to Upland (acres)	Changed to Other PVEG Types (acres)	Changed to Pond/Deepwater (acres)
PEM	12.15	6.46	9.31
PFO	3.03	.00	0.74
PSS	0.15	.00	0.48
TOTAL	15.33	6.46	10.53

2. Causes of Palustrine Vegetated Wetland Loss to Upland:

Agriculture (9.88 acres), Housing (2.43), Commercial/Industrial Development (1.33), Roads (1.26), and Marina (0.43).

3. Types Most Converted to Upland:

PEM, Temporarily Flooded (6.73 acres); PEM, Seasonally Flooded (5.43 acres)

4. Gains in PVEG Wetlands from Upland:

36.24 acres (all PEM)

5. New Pond Acreage Created:

65.24 (54.71 from Upland; 10.53 from Wetland)

WETLAND TRENDS STUDY HIGHLIGHTS - **PENNSYLVANIA**

STUDY AREA:

Williamsport area - 2 Quads (Muncy and Montoursville North)

STUDY PERIOD: 1977 to 1988/90

MAJOR FINDINGS:

1. Changes in Vegetated Wetlands:

Wetland Type	Converted to Upland (acres)	Changed to Other PVEG Types (acres)	Changed to Pond/Deepwater (acres)
PEM	1.77	2.07	.00
PFO	2.58	.00	1.11
TOTAL	4.35	2.07	1.11

2. Causes of Palustrine Vegetated Wetland Loss to Upland:

Agriculture (2.00), Ditching (1.04), Recreational Facility (0.79), and Unknown (0.52).

3. New Pond Acreage Created:

12.6 (11.49 from Upland; 1.11 from Wetland)

WETLAND TRENDS STUDY HIGHLIGHTS - **PENNSYLVANIA**

STUDY AREA:

   Hazelton Quad

STUDY PERIOD: 1981 to 1987

MAJOR FINDINGS:

1.   Changes in Vegetated Wetlands:

Wetland Type	Converted to Upland (acres)	Changed to Other PVEG Types (acres)	Changed to Pond/Deepwater (acres)
PEM	2.29	.00	.00
PFO	.00	9.68	11.30
PSS	1.78	.00	.00
TOTAL	4.07	9.68	11.30

2.   Causes of Palustrine Vegetated Wetland Loss to Upland:

   Recreational Facility (1.78), Roads (1.48), and Reservoir (0.81).

3.   New Pond Acreage Created:

   30.37 (from Upland)

WETLAND TRENDS STUDY HIGHLIGHTS - **PENNSYLVANIA**

STUDY AREA:

DuBois and Falls Creek Quads

STUDY PERIOD: 1983 to 1988

MAJOR FINDINGS:

1. Changes in Vegetated Wetlands:

Wetland Type	Converted to Upland (acres)	Changed to Other PVEG Types (acres)	Changed to Pond/Deepwater (acres)
PEM	0.86	1.06	0.20
PFO	.00	1.82	2.01
PSS	.00	2.66	.00
TOTAL	0.86	5.54	2.21

2. Causes of Palustrine Vegetated Wetland Loss to Upland:

   Mining (0.45 acres) and Roads (0.41).

3. Type Most Converted to Upland:

   PEM

4. Gains in PVEG Wetlands from Upland:

   8.69 acres

5. New Pond Acreage Created:

   26.39 (24.18 from Upland; 2.21 from Wetland)